SpringerBriefs in Computer Science

SpringerBriefs present concise summaries of cutting-edge research and practical applications across a wide spectrum of fields. Featuring compact volumes of 50 to 125 pages, the series covers a range of content from professional to academic.

Typical topics might include:

- A timely report of state-of-the art analytical techniques
- A bridge between new research results, as published in journal articles, and a contextual literature review
- A snapshot of a hot or emerging topic
- An in-depth case study or clinical example
- A presentation of core concepts that students must understand in order to make independent contributions

Briefs allow authors to present their ideas and readers to absorb them with minimal time investment. Briefs will be published as part of Springer's eBook collection, with millions of users worldwide. In addition, Briefs will be available for individual print and electronic purchase. Briefs are characterized by fast, global electronic dissemination, standard publishing contracts, easy-to-use manuscript preparation and formatting guidelines, and expedited production schedules. We aim for publication 8–12 weeks after acceptance. Both solicited and unsolicited manuscripts are considered for publication in this series.

**Indexing: This series is indexed in Scopus, Ei-Compendex, and zbMATH **

Kaisong Huang • Tianzheng Wang

Indexing on
Non-Volatile Memory

Techniques, Lessons Learned and Outlook

 Springer

Kaisong Huang
Simon Fraser University
Burnaby, BC, Canada

Tianzheng Wang
Simon Fraser University
Burnaby, BC, Canada

ISSN 2191-5768 ISSN 2191-5776 (electronic)
SpringerBriefs in Computer Science
ISBN 978-3-031-47626-6 ISBN 978-3-031-47627-3 (eBook)
https://doi.org/10.1007/978-3-031-47627-3

This Springer imprint is published by the registered company Springer Nature Switzerland AG
The registered company address is: Gewerbestrasse 11, 6330 Cham, Switzerland

Paper in this product is recyclable.

Preface

As DRAM scaling stalls, it becomes ever important to find alternatives. A promising direction is scalable, byte-addressable non-volatile memory (NVM). NVM combines the benefits of both memory and storage, to offer byte-addressability like DRAM while scaling well to provide high capacity that rivals that of HDDs and flash SSDs. There are many different types of NVM devices with different performance, cost and energy profiles; many of them offer much better energy profile compared to DRAM and even SRAM. They are in general expected to be more cost-effective than DRAM, albeit typically being more expensive than flash memory which is widely used today to build SSDs. For example, the performance and cost of phase change memory (PCM) and Intel 3D XPoint (Optane) sit right in between DRAM and flash memory, while STT-RAM has the potential of replacing or complementing SRAM to build better CPU caches that are energy-efficient and high-performance. These promising features have led to many interesting proposals in the database systems and broader computer systems communities since early 2000s. Despite being discontinued due to various reasons (which we try to explore later in this book), the commercialization of Optane in 2019 further spurred more interests in this area while newer devices such as Nano-RAM and STT-RAM are being actively studied.

NVM can fundamentally change the design of almost all DBMS components, especially logging, buffer management, indexing and query execution. Among these, indexes play key roles in OLTP and OLAP systems to deliver high performance and have arguably received the most attention from both academia and industry. With byte-addressability and persistence on the memory bus, an NVM-based index can operate and persist data directly on NVM, without heavyweight I/O operations going through the file system and I/O stacks like traditional disk-based indexes. These indexes can also provide (near) instant recovery to greatly improve system availability. Since most of these NVM devices scale much better than DRAM and do so at a lower cost than DRAM, they also provide an excellent approach to high-capacity (although slower) memory that can potentially ease storage bottlenecks and allow previously prohibitively expensive systems—such as main-memory DBMSs—to become practical by storing in-memory indexes or buffering data in cheap NVM.

This book focuses on OLTP indexes designed for NVM and provides a systematic review and summary of the fundamental principles and techniques and outlook for this area. Part of this book is based on the authors' past publications. Readers may find materials from these previous publications reprinted in this book with permission, and we always encourage interested readers to check out the original papers for more detailed discussions.

In this book, we divide the development of NVM indexes into three "eras"— pre-Optane, Optane and post-Optane—based on when the first major scalable NVM device (Optane) became commercially available and when it was announced to be discontinued. The book will also analyze the reasons for the slow adoption of NVM and give an outlook for indexing techniques in the post-Optane era.

We hope the techniques described in this book will not only benefit practitioners who want to build NVM-based systems, but can also inspire new designs for DRAM (in-memory) and SSD/disk-based indexes. The usefulness of this book will also go beyond particular indexing techniques, by discussing NVM hardware and software issues in general, which can be informative for the broad computer systems community. The book will only assume basic undergraduate-level understanding on indexing (e.g., B+-trees, hash tables) and database systems in general. This book is otherwise self-contained with the necessary background information, including an introduction to NVM hardware and software/programming issues, a detailed description of different indexes in highly concurrent systems for non-experts and new researchers to get started in this area.

Vancouver, Canada   *Kaisong Huang*
Vancouver, Canada   *Tianzheng Wang*
July 2023

Contents

Chapter 1
Introduction

Abstract This chapter gives an introduction to the topics covered by this book, in particular the overall vision of byte-addressable non-volatile memory (NVM) and its impact on database indexing.

1.1 The Non-Volatile Memory Vision

In a traditional storage hierarchy, "memory" serves as the intermediary between CPU and secondary storage which is the permanent home of data. Persistent data must be deserialized and transformed into memory format for CPU to use. Dynamic random access memory (DRAM) has virtually been the only memory medium in modern computer systems. It is volatile but offers low access latency (50-100ns) that fills the gap between storage (HDDs and SSDs) and CPU caches built with SRAM. In recent years, advances in manufacturing have led to continued increase in capacity and drop in price of DRAM; some high-end servers can feature 100s of GBs or TBs of DRAM-based main memory [7]. This has made memory-centric computing [3] possible where the working set can fit in memory, removing the need to access storage on the critical path that is orders of magnitudes slower.

DRAM scaling, however, is ending [1], which makes it difficult to build DRAM chips that offer high capacity. DRAM is also inherently much more expensive than SSDs and HDDs, and unlike the latter, the price of DRAM DIMMs does not scale linearly with capacity. For example, the unit price of a 128GB DDR4 DRAM DIMM is beyond twice the price of a 32GB DDR4 DIMM of the same model [9]. Therefore, as of this writing (2023 H1), it is still rare to see 128GB or larger DRAM DIMMs being deployed in real systems. Instead, most mainstream servers use 16–64GB DIMMs to balance cost and capacity. Equipping more DRAM in a server also means higher power and energy consumption. Prior work [4] has discovered that DRAM alone could consume as much as 46% of the total system power.

These issues motivated computer architects and hardware designers to find alternatives to DRAM that scale (for higher capacity) and/or consume less energy while

© The Author(s), under exclusive license to Springer Nature Switzerland AG 2024

K. Huang, T. Wang, *Indexing on Non-Volatile Memory*, SpringerBriefs in Computer Science, https://doi.org/10.1007/978-3-031-47627-3_1

providing competitive performance to DRAM. A variety of such alternatives, e.g., phase change memory (PCM) [21], spin-torque transfer RAM (STT-RAM) [8] and memristor [20] have emerged, thanks to advances in material sciences. Although they exhibit different properties in terms of performance and energy profiles, most (if not all) of them—perhaps coincidentally—are also non-volatile. That is, unlike DRAM which requires constant power to maintain data, data stored on such *non-volatile memory* (NVM)[1] devices can survive power cycles. As a result, in addition to having better energy profiles, NVM combines the best of SSDs/HDDs (by being capacious and persistence) and DRAM (by being byte-addressable), blurring the boundary between memory and storage.

The combination of non-volatility and byte-addressability opens up many opportunities to build high-performance computer systems where NVM can sit on the memory bus to replace or complement normal DRAM. Even secondary storage could potentially become obsolete with high-capacity NVM, leading to *single-level* stores that consist of only NVM outside the CPU. Software data structures can directly operate and persist data using normal `load` and `store` instructions on the memory bus without having to go through the file system and I/O stacks, saving serialization and format conversion costs. Reducing the number of layers also helps with simplifying software design, which in turn eases debugging, testing and maintenance. Moreover, as many data processing tasks move to memory-centric designs, without expensive I/O operations, database systems could benefit from such single-level designs and NVM to provide instant recovery, low-latency commit and fast persistence. Among the various components in a database system, indexes can especially attain these benefits, as we will elaborate in the rest of this book.

NVM, however, is not perfect. Compared to DRAM, the main drawbacks are that they typically (although not always) have limited endurance, higher access latency and lower bandwidth. For example, as one of the most mature candidate NVM, PCM can be $\sim$3–5$\times$ slower than DRAM and wear out after 10^8–10^9 programming cycles (in contrast to DRAM's over 10^{16} programming cycles) [12]. Other alternatives, such as STT-RAM, could rival SRAM in terms of latency, but still face major challenges in scalability and data retention. There have been significant advances at the hardware level that improve these aspects of NVM [12, 18, 19, 22], but the only commercial product that truly scales to high capacity (in the order of TBs) is Intel Optane Persistent Memory (PMem) [10, 11] which unfortunately is being wound down as of this writing. As pointed out by recent work [9], the overall cost per performance (in terms of bandwidth) of Optane PMem is in fact even higher than SSDs for index workloads. This makes it hard for Optane PMem to get adopted widely in real deployments. We will explore its impact and give outlook in the final chapter, however, the techniques discussed in this book apply beyond Optane PMem, even to traditional DRAM and SSD-based systems.

---

[1] Also known as non-volatile RAM (NVRAM), storage class memory (SCM) or persistent memory (PM). In this book, we use these terms interchangeably to refer to memory devices that are byte-addressable *and* non-volatile. In the literature, flash memory (although usually not byte-addressable) is also sometimes referred to as "NVM" which should not be confused with the focus of this book.

1.2 Database Indexing on NVM

A major goal of database systems is to well use memory and storage to balance cost and performance. To this end, traditional storage-centric database systems typically employ a buffer pool to cache data and changes to data are stored permanently on secondary storage [6]. As we have briefly mentioned earlier, the dropping DRAM price and increasing DRAM space allowed memory-optimized database systems where the working set or even entire databases can fit in memory, leading to a series of changes done to core database engine components that remove unnecessary overheads and drastically improve performance [2]. Instead of using a buffer pool, these systems directly allocate data records in main memory (on the heap) and use virtual memory pointers to access data, saving much indirection overhead incurred by traditional buffer pools. On top of this, main-memory indexes [13, 15, 16] are widely used to optimize data access paths: they directly map keys to addresses or logical record IDs of data records in memory. These indexes are highly optimized versions of traditional indexes, such as B+-trees, tries and hash tables. Consequently, they provide a set of common operations, including insert, point read (retrieving the value(s) mapped by one key), update, delete and range scan. We will give details of these main-memory indexes along with their key optimizations in Chapter 3.

From a high level, contrary to indexes in traditional storage-centric systems, indexes in main-memory database systems are often volatile and need to be rebuilt upon restart, reducing service availability. Although in storage-centric database systems, indexes are permanently stored in SSDs/HDDs, they are subject to the afore-mentioned buffer management overhead. NVM fills this gap nicely, by providing immediate persistence to indexes such that upon restart the index is readily available for transactions and queries to use. Compared to SSDs and hard disks, NVM is expected to perform at least an order of magnitude better (with lower latency and/or higher bandwidth), which makes it desirable to use NVM (instead of SSDs or HDDs) to store indexes for higher performance.

Realizing such NVM vision for indexes requires careful (re)design of the indexes to cope with NVM's properties. There are three main design questions:

- **Q1:** What is NVM's role, i.e., which properties (high capacity, persistence, byte-addressability and low power consumption) of NVM are being leveraged?
- **Q2:** How should NVM be accessed, given NVM is both memory (load/store instructions) and storage (block I/O)?
- **Q3:** With Q1 and Q2 settled, how should indexes be designed to best benefit from NVM yet mitigating its drawbacks mentioned in Section 1.1?

Q1 and Q2 are in fact general questions whose answers go beyond indexing and database systems. NVM's role still remains an open problem given the wide range of devices which have different properties. Arguably, it is likely that NVM will be (and indeed is, for the commercially available Optane PMem) a complement to DRAM and flash SSDs. This leads to two possible ways of using NVM: (a) as larger but slower memory (with DRAM as a transparent "L4 cache"), or (b) as permanent storage side-by-side with DRAM. Note that one could potentially combine the two approaches, by using certain NVM space as a cache and the remaining as byte-addressable storage. Most (if not all) NVM-based indexes so far have opted for the second approach, as it allows software (index) to judiciously use NVM to store index structures (e.g., B+-tree nodes) and control data movement explicitly. The two approaches also directly map to Intel Optane PMem's two operating modes (Memory and AppDirect) [10] which we elaborate later. In the rest of the book, we will also focus on techniques proposed assuming the second approach and using `load`/`store` instructions to directly access data on NVM.

While NVM is persistent, the CPU caches—which `load`/`store` instructions usually must go through—may not be persistent as they are built in SRAM and not all the processors on the market are equipped with techniques like extended asynchronous refresh domain (eADR) [11] or whole system persistence [17]. Overcoming this issue constitutes a main design challenge for NVM indexes (Q3), which must explicit issue cacheline flush instructions (e.g., `CLFLUSH`/`CLFLUSHOPT`/`CLWB`) to ensure data reaches NVM. In addition, indexes must also account for the fact that NVM may be slower than DRAM to reduce unnecessary NVM reads and writes. Finally, the first commercially available NVM device (Optane PMem) further exhibited a few unique properties that were not considered before by indexes (even those built specifically for NVM, because real NVM devices were not available at all). This further led to more careful designs required, e.g., despite being byte-addressable to software, the internal access granularity of Optane is in fact 256-byte; indexes must account for this fact to carefully issue reads and writes.

The majority of work so far on NVM indexing has assumed that NVM is slower than DRAM, but faster than SSDs. However, certain NVM candidates, such as STT-RAM, have the potential of being faster than DRAM (in terms of offering lower latency and/or higher bandwidth). They are largely still work-in-progress, and so has not gained much traction in software design. We expect future work to reconsider index designs with scalable NVM that rivals SRAM/DRAM performance.

With the architecture choice clarified (Q1), starting from the next chapter, we will give an overview of the NVM landscape, introduce how it is programmed (Q2), before surveying recent techniques for NVM indexing (Q3). Finally, we distill a set of design principles and present an analysis of these techniques and give an outlook for future work. Note that the focus of this book is on the design principles of NVM indexing, instead of empirical performance evaluations of NVM indexes for which we refer readers to other work [5, 14].

References

[1] Process integration, devices & structures. International Technology Roadmap for Semiconductors (2007)
[2] Faerber, F., Kemper, A., Åke Larson, P., Levandoski, J., Neumann, T., Pavlo, A.: Main Memory Database Systems. Foundations and Trends® in Databases **8**(1-2), 1–130 (2017)

[3] Gebregiorgis, A., Du Nguyen, H.A., Yu, J., Bishnoi, R., Taouil, M., Catthoor, F., Hamdioui, S.: A Survey on Memory-Centric Computer Architectures. J. Emerg. Technol. Comput. Syst. **18**(4) (2022)

[4] Ghose, S., Yaglikçi, A.G., Gupta, R., Lee, D., Kudrolli, K., Liu, W.X., Hassan, H., Chang, K.K., Chatterjee, N., Agrawal, A., O'Connor, M., Mutlu, O.: What Your DRAM Power Models Are Not Telling You: Lessons from a Detailed Experimental Study. Proc. ACM Meas. Anal. Comput. Syst. **2**(3) (2018)

[5] He, Y., Lu, D., Huang, K., Wang, T.: Evaluating Persistent Memory Range Indexes: Part Two. Proc. VLDB Endow. **15**(11), 2477–2490 (2022)

[6] Hellerstein, J.M., Stonebraker, M., Hamilton, J.: Architecture of a Database System. Found. Trends Databases **1**(2), 141–259 (2007)

[7] Hewlett Packard Enterprise: HPE Integrity Superdome X Server. URL https://support.hpe.com/hpesc/public/docDisplay?docId=c04402500\&docLocale=en_US

[8] Hosomi, M., Yamagishi, H., Yamamoto, T., Bessho, K., Higo, Y., Yamane, K., Yamada, H., Shoji, M., Hachino, H., Fukumoto, C., Nagao, H., Kano, H.: A novel nonvolatile memory with spin torque transfer magnetization switching: Spin-RAM pp. 459–462 (2005)

[9] Huang, K., Imai, D., Wang, T., Xie, D.: SSDs Striking Back: The Storage Jungle and Its Implications on Persistent Indexes. In: 12th Annual Conference on Innovative Data Systems Research, CIDR 2022, Chaminade, CA, USA, January 9-12, 2022, Online Proceedings (2022)

[10] Intel Corporation: Brief: Intel Optane Persistent Memory (2021). URL https://www.intel.ca/content/www/ca/en/products/docs/memory-storage/optane-persistent-memory/optane-dc-persistent-memory-brief.html

[11] Intel Corporation: Intel Optane Persistent Memory 200 series brief (2022). URL https://www.intel.ca/content/www/ca/en/products/docs/memory-storage/optane-persistent-memory/optane-persistent-memory-200-series-brief.html

[12] Lee, B.C., Ipek, E., Mutlu, O., Burger, D.: Architecting Phase Change Memory as a Scalable Dram Alternative. In: Proceedings of the 36th Annual International Symposium on Computer Architecture, ISCA '09, p. 2–13. Association for Computing Machinery, New York, NY, USA (2009)

[13] Leis, V., Kemper, A., Neumann, T.: The Adaptive Radix Tree: ARTful Indexing for Main-Memory Databases. In: Proceedings of the 2013 IEEE International Conference on Data Engineering, ICDE '13, p. 38–49 (2013)

[14] Lersch, L., Hao, X., Oukid, I., Wang, T., Willhalm, T.: Evaluating Persistent Memory Range Indexes. PVLDB **13**(4), 574–587 (2019)

[15] Levandoski, J.J., Lomet, D.B., Sengupta, S.: The Bw-Tree: A B-tree for new hardware platforms. In: Proceedings of the 2013 IEEE International Conference on Data Engineering (ICDE 2013), ICDE '13, pp. 302–313 (2013)

[16] Mao, Y., Kohler, E., Morris, R.T.: Cache Craftiness for Fast Multicore Key-Value Storage. In: Proceedings of the 7th ACM european conference on Computer Systems, pp. 183–196 (2012)

[17] Narayanan, D., Hodson, O.: Whole-System Persistence. In: Proceedings of the Seventeenth International Conference on Architectural Support for Programming Languages and Operating Systems, ASPLOS XVII, p. 401–410. Association for Computing Machinery, New York, NY, USA (2012)

[18] Qureshi, M.K., Karidis, J., Franceschini, M., Srinivasan, V., Lastras, L., Abali, B.: Enhancing Lifetime and Security of PCM-Based Main Memory with Start-Gap Wear Leveling. In: Proceedings of the 42nd Annual IEEE/ACM International Symposium on Microarchitecture, MICRO 42, p. 14–23 (2009)

[19] Song, S., Das, A., Mutlu, O., Kandasamy, N.: Improving Phase Change Memory Performance with Data Content Aware Access. In: Proceedings of the 2020 ACM SIGPLAN International Symposium on Memory Management, ISMM 2020, p. 30–47 (2020)

[20] Strukov, D.B., Snider, G.S., Stewart, D.R., Williams, R.S.: The missing memristor found. Nature **453**(7191), 80–83 (2008)

[21] Wong, H.S.P., Raoux, S., Kim, S., Liang, J., Reifenberg, J.P., Rajendran, B., Asheghi, M., Goodson, K.E.: Phase change memory. Proceedings of the IEEE **98**(12), 2201–2227 (2010)

[22] Zhou, P., Zhao, B., Yang, J., Zhang, Y.: A Durable and Energy Efficient Main Memory Using Phase Change Memory Technology. In: Proceedings of the 36th Annual International Symposium on Computer Architecture, ISCA '09, p. 14–23. Association for Computing Machinery, New York, NY, USA (2009)

Chapter 2
NVM Hardware and Software

Abstract This chapter provides the necessary background on NVM hardware, how it fits in modern computer systems and the way software can program it.

2.1 Non-Volatile Memory Hardware Landscape

The term "NVM" can refer to a very broad range of devices in the DIMM form factor and that are both (1) byte-addressable *and* (2) non-volatile. Various devices have been proposed to realize this vision, using either traditional or new materials, along with advanced manufacturing technologies. The variety of hardware techniques led to a variety of performance characteristics, device lifetime and energy profiles. Based on their maturity, we introduce representative NVM technologies below. We focus on the devices' overall properties and their impact to software; more low-level hardware details is beyond the scope of this book and can be found elsewhere as noted in the reference list of this chapter.

2.1.1 Maturing and In-Production NVM Devices

We begin with three maturing/in-production NVM devices, including phase change memory, 3D XPoint (Intel Optane PMem) and NVDIMMs.

Phase Change Memory (PCM)

PCM [49] has almost been synonymous of NVM in NVM indexing and related areas. PCM stores data by changing the physical state of the underlying material—which most commonly is $Ge_2Sb_2Te_5$ (GST) [7]—between amorphous and crystalline states that respectively exhibit high (logic zero) and low resistance (logic one) levels. Such transition is done by applying current and heat in different ways to GST; more details about the making PCM chips can be found elsewhere [39]; we focus on PCM's overall properties and their implications to software.

Compared to DRAM, PCM exhibits higher latency, limited endurance of 10^8–10^9 programming cycles (whereas the number for DRAM is at least 10^{15}) [29]. PCM also exhibits asymmetric read and write latencies, with writes being longer [29]. At both the hardware and software levels, numerous caching and wear levelling approaches have been proposed to devise PCM as a viable alternative or complement of DRAM, by improving its performance and/or endurance [12, 29, 35, 40, 51]. This is still an open research area in the hardware and architecture communities today. Many vendors, including Intel, Micron, Samsung and IBM [4], have all started to work on PCM since very early stage and some have announced sample chips as early as 2012 [1] but those were typically limited to low capacity (e.g., 1Gb or 128MB).

3D XPoint (Optane PMem)

Intel and Micron announced the 3D XPoint [13] technology in 2015 which—as third-party analyses report—uses the aforementioned PCM. As the first commercially available NVM that truly scales (available in 128GB, 256GB and 512GB DIMMs), the Intel Optane DC Persistent Memory (DCPMM, later renamed to Optane PMem) devices are based on 3D XPoint and exhibit many similarities to PCM. However, the full internal of Optane PMem remains trade secret. Its performance generally falls between DRAM and flash, with asymmetric read and write latency (with reads being faster in general at the device level). Although it is not clear how Optane PMem internally enhances endurance (e.g., using wear levelling algorithms), the manufacturer guarantees the device will not break within its warranty period of five years [24, 25, 31], which is also the typical device lifecyle in modern data centres. This practically eliminates the need for software wear levelling techniques, allowing software systems to focus more on designing for performance and functionality.

Performance-wise, Optane PMem behaves differently than many assumptions made by software before they became available as prior assumptions (1) were mostly based on PCM and (2) had to use emulation which does not have the enough level of details. Specifically, the first generation of PMem (Optane DCPMM 100 series) exhibits ~300ns read latency (~4× higher than DRAM's ~75ns latency). Its bandwidth is also ~3–14× lower than DDR4 DRAM and asymmetric by offering different peak sequential read (40GB/s), sequential write bandwidth (10GB/s), random read (~7.4GB/s) and random write (~5.3GB/s) bandwidth [24, 30]. Similar to using DRAM DIMMs, multiple DIMMs can be used to obtain higher aggregate bandwidth. With more memory channel support from newer CPU generations, the later Optane PMem 200 and 300 series products offer roughly 30% higher bandwidth [25]. However, configuring a machine with Optane PMem DIMMs comes with multiple restrictions and requires specific (higher end) Intel CPUs which potentially contributed to the slow adoption and eventual winding down of Optane products [21]; we will expand on more detail later. In addition to these basic performance numbers, multiple efforts further discovered the idiosyncrasies of Optane PMem [18, 26, 36, 50]. Among the findings, it is particularly notable that (1) Optane bandwidth is a scarce resource, (2) although it is in DDR form factor and byte-addressable, the device has an internal access granularity of 256 bytes. As a result, writes smaller than 256 bytes may incur write amplification, similar to flash memory which usually has a fixed page size of several KBs. These properties significantly affects how software (indexes in our case) should be designed to achieve reasonable performance. We provide more details in later chapter when discussing "Optane-era" NVM indexes.

Non-Volatile DIMMs

Astute readers may have already realized that by definition, "NVM" could be built even without any new materials, but with DRAM and battery/supercapacitors. This leads to the so-called non-volatile DIMMs (NVDIMMs), which are perhaps the most mature NVM technology and have been on the market very early on.[1] The basic idea is to back volatile DRAM with flash and battery/supercapacitor, such that with power, the device behaves exactly the same as normal DRAM. However, upon power failure, the device will store the DRAM contents to flash memory using the energy provided by the battery/supercapacitor. When power resumes, data is again loaded back from flash memory to DRAM to resume normal operation; the battery/supercapacitor is also recharged for future use. Multiple vendors have released real NVDIMM products [5, 45] and commercial database management systems like Microsoft SQL Server have adopted them for logging to provide low-latency commit [32].

NVDIMMs are standardized with multiple versions by the Storage Networking Industry Association (SNIA) according to the amount of and the way DRAM and flash are used [44]. For example, NVDIMM-N uses equal amounts of DRAM and flash memory, and the latter is only used as a "safety net" to ensure durability of data on DRAM upon power failure. With more flash memory, NVDIMM-F can present to the user much larger (but slower) memory and use the smaller DRAM as a transparent cache. NVDIMM-N was a main research vehicle for NVM software research [6, 47, 48] before Optane PMem became commercially available. However, its performance characteristics are very different than Optane PMem's, by exhibiting exactly the same performance of DRAM during normal operation, making earlier software proposals that base on NVDIMMs less applicable to "real" NVM such as Optane PMem.

---

[1] Technically, "NVDIMM" could be used interchangeably with "NVM" in this book as the name only suggests non-volatility and the DIMM form factor, which do not necessarily indicate the underlying material (new scalable materials like PCM or DRAM) used to build it. However, in most literature NVDIMM specifically refers to those devices built using traditional technologies like DRAM and flash with supercapacitors. We also follow this convention throughout this book.

2.1.2 Work-In-Progress NVM Candidates

Beyond PCM, Optane and NVDIMMs, other candidates for NVM are also being explored. They hold the same "byte-addressable and non-volatile" promise as
PCM/Optane and NVDIMMs do, but can exhibit quite different performance and
energy profiles. We give an overview of several notable technologies, including
memristor, STT-RAM and NanoTube RAM. However, note that the list here is by no
means exhaustive and the area is progressing quickly.

Memristor

Dubbed as the "fourth basic circuit element," memristor [41] stores information by
changing its resistance level as current passes through its two layers of titanium
dioxide and wire electrodes. Compared to the aforementioned candidates, memristor
has the potential of achieving very low latencies at the pico-second or tens of
nanosecond levels. This makes it an idea candidate to even serve as a replacement or
complement for SRAM which is currently only used to build CPU caches due to its
high cost. Hewlett Packard (and later Hewlett Packard Enterprise) was a major force
driving this effort by announcing the "The Machine" project in 2014. The vision was
to provide a single-level NVM-based system that "fuses memory and storage" [19]
which would allow applications to dispose of traditional storage hierarchies and be
simplified with only memory accesses. The NVM component in The Machine was
planned to be memristor, which however, was not successful in terms of providing
the needed scalability (capacity) and performance before HPE pivoted to using
traditional DRAM for a proof-of-concept [2] of The Machine. Nevertheless, the The
Machine project left much legacy in NVM research, for example on providing support
for programming NVM [8, 10] and on how to leverage NVM in database systems [28].
It also included revolutionary ideas around massively parallel, manycore processors
and interconnects, part of which helped shape future interconnects [3, 33]; details
around these aspects are beyond the scope of this book, interested readers may refer
to the references at the end of this chapter.

STT-RAM

Spin-transfer torque (magnetic) RAM (STT-RAM/STT-MRAM) [20] leverages the
spin-transfer torque property where the orientation of a magnetic layer can be ma-
nipulated using polarizing current to store data. It consists of one magnetic junction
and one transistor, and is expected to be very scalable, durable and fast (comparable
to SRAM). In addition, it offers much better energy profile compared to traditional
SRAM and DRAM, allowing the potential of replacing or complementing SRAM as
the CPU cache. Everspin [14] has released STT-MRAM products and Intel [43] has
demonstrated STT-RAM as L4 cache. Some research also has investigated the possi-
bility of relaxing certain properties (e.g., data retention) in exchange for even higher

performance and better energy behaviour [27, 42]. However, to date its capacity is still limited and STT-RAM with high capacity (that rivals DRAM and flash) is not yet in mass production compared to Optane PMem.

Nano-RAM

Nano-RAM (NRAM) uses carbon nanotubes deposited on a chip-like substrate to store data [34]. Carbon nanotube's small size (1/50,000th the diameter of a human hair) allows it to scale well to large capacity [34]. It also offers high performance (full speed of DRAM) and low power consumption [16]. It is currently a proprietary technology being developed by Nantero [17] and is again, yet to see widespread commercial use.

2.2 System Architecture

With background on individual NVM devices, now we discuss how they can be integrated in a system at the hardware level.

2.2.1 NVM in the Storage Hierarchy

As can be seen from our discussion in Section 2.1, the hardware landscape of NVM is both uniform and diverse. On the one hand, it is "uniform" because except NVDIMMs, they all offer non-volatility, byte-addressability, good scalability (high capacity) and low power consumption (at least in theory) when compared to DRAM.[2] On the other hand, it is very diverse because different NVM devices use different underlying materials and their (potential) performance differs much from each other. Some (e.g., STT-RAM) can compete with SRAM and have the potential of being the ideal NVM that replaces SRAM, DRAM and even flash memory, while some (e.g., PCM and 3D XPoint) offer performance characteristics right in between DRAM and flash memory. This impacts how NVM may fit in the memory hierarchy of today's von Neumann architecture. With ultra-fast NVM that rivals SRAM and DRAM performance yet with flash-level capacity, the entire memory hierarchy could be "flattened" or still maintain as a hierarchy but with new NVM replacing the current technology used in each existing tier. For example, there have been attempts in leveraging fast NVM to build persistent CPU caches in the context of "normally off, instant on" computing [15]. However, they are still limited by the existing underlying technology's scalability, and are far from commercial use in large-scale data management workloads.

---

[2] NVDIMMs usually lack scalability (NVDIMM-N) and/or fall short on power consumption as they rely on traditional DRAM.

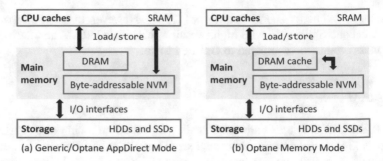

Fig. 2.1: Architectures of today's NVM-based systems, assuming NVM's performance is between DRAM and flash SSDs. NVM is placed side-by-side with DRAM in DIMM slots but can be used in different ways by software. (a) Software uses load/store instructions to explicitly access and determine data placement on NVM and DRAM. This corresponds to the "AppDirect" mode of Optane PMem. (b) DRAM serves as a (transparent) cache of NVM, presenting software larger but slower memory ("Memory" mode of Optane PMem). A third hybrid architecture that may combine (a) and (b) which is omitted here for brevity. Most NVM indexes assume (a) as it allows more flexibility and more room for performance optimizations.

The most mature/in-production NVM technologies today fit right between DRAM and flash. Although it is possible to architect a system where such NVM is the only device on the memory bus (forming an SRAM-NVM-SSD architecture), in practice this offers much worse performance than a traditional SRAM-DRAM-SSD system because existing maturing/in-production NVM is still slower than DRAM (e.g., Optane PMem is ~3–5× slower than DRAM as we mentioned earlier). Therefore, it is reasonable to assume a revised memory hierarchy where DRAM and NVM co-exist; a revisit would be necessary if the next commercially available NVM offers very different performance characteristics. In this revised memory hierarchy, NVM DIMMs are located on the memory bus, side-by-side with DRAM DIMMs, as shown in Figure 2.1. However, both NVM and DRAM are behind multiple levels of CPU caches, which are still built using SRAM, instead of the aforementioned NVM technologies. Also, both NVM and DRAM are addressable by software using memory instructions, such as load/store.

2.2.2 Role of NVM

Starting from this section, we base our discussions mostly on today's NVM (e.g., Optane PMem) whose performance characteristics fall between DRAM and flash SSDs. Thus, we consider the aforementioned architectures with both DRAM and NVM on the memory bus. It then becomes important to determine the role of them and provide support at the hardware level. In general, given DRAM is faster, it can be used as a cache or tier to mitigate the performance impact of storing indexes fully on NVM, while maintaining the benefits (large capacity and/or persistence) brought by using NVM. This led to two major ways of using DRAM and NVM in the memory/storage hierarchy.

Generic DRAM-NVM Architecture

Figure 2.1(a) shows what we refer to as the "generic" approach where NVM and DRAM are directly accessible by software using memory instructions. Software (e.g., database indexes) assuming this approach then can judiciously determine data placement and determine the role of DRAM to optimize for performance. For example, some NVM indexes place frequently-used but reconstructible tree nodes in DRAM and the remaining nodes in NVM to accelerate lookups. In the context of actual NVM products, this approach corresponds to the "AppDirect" mode of Optane PMem and gives the most flexibility for software to leverage all the properties of NVM (especially persistence and byte-addressability).

Note that the generic architecture was already the assumed architecture before Optane PMem became available. Almost all research in NVM software (including indexes) assumes this approach and attempts to match the performance of a DRAM-based system with NVM and a small amount of DRAM as a cache or a tier.

DRAM as a Transparent Cache

Another approach is using DRAM as a *transparent* cache to NVM, as represented by the "Memory" mode of Optane PMem shown in Figure 2.1(b). Currently this is a Optane-specific feature done at the hardware level. It presents software larger but slower *volatile* memory without persistence, leveraging NVM's large capacity. Compared to the AppDirect mode under which software may also use DRAM as a cache with customized caching policies, the caching policy in Memory mode is controlled by hardware (memory controller). This forbids software from explicitly controlling data placement (on DRAM or NVM), but offers very easy adoption as no change in software is needed (of course, they still must use secondary storage such as SSDs to store data permanently). In contrast, the generic/AppDirect mode typically would require redesigning software to fully utilize NVM.

Hybrid Modes

Instead of choosing between the above two approaches, one could also mix and match to use certain portions of DRAM and NVM for each mode, leading to the "Hybrid" setup in the context of Optane PMem.

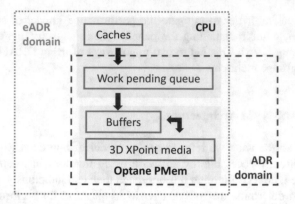

Fig. 2.2: Persistence domains of Optane PMem based systems. Since the first generation of Optane PMem, data is considered persistent once it reaches the ADR domain
(not necessarily NVM), i.e., after a cacheline flush/eviction event. The extended
ADR (eADR) feature in later generations further includes the entire CPU cache in
the ADR domain, practically providing persistent CPU caches and removing the
need for proactively issuing cacheline flushes by software.

2.3 Programming Model

Most (if not all) NVM indexing proposals focus on leveraging the generic approach
(Optane's AppDirect mode) because it allows software to fully extract the potential
of NVM. This is the assumption of the rest of this book, unless otherwise specified. Programming the new hierarchy requires support from both the hardware and
software levels.

Hardware Support

From a very high-level, since the CPU cache is still volatile (SRAM) and there is
still a large speed gap between existing NVM and SRAM/DRAM, it is necessary to
well leverage the CPU cache and subsequently, ensure that any data modifications
done in the CPU cache are properly persisted in NVM. This requires software
proactively issue cacheline flush instructions (CLFLUSH, CLFLUSHOPT and CLWB in
Intel CPUs [22]) after writing NVM-backed memory blocks. Moreover, to cope
with memory reordering done by the CPU, software must also issue fences (such
as SFENCE in Intel CPUs) between consecutive NVM accesses. Figure 2.2 shows
how a store or cacheline flush is handled by Optane PMem, the only NVM device
in mass production. When data is forced out of the CPU cache (as a result of
the software proactively issuing a cacheline flush instruction or a CPU-initiated
cacheline eviction), the memory controller places the data in a write pending queue,
which is then drained later for data to reach the actual Optane DIMMs. Since the

first generation of Optane PMem, the write pending queue and PMem DIMMs are included in the asynchronous DRAM refresh (ADR) domain where data is guaranteed to survive power cycles. That is, data in the write pending queue is guaranteed to be drained within a "hold-up" time of $100\mu s$ [37]. As a result, after the software issues a cacheline flush instruction which forces the data to the CPU's write pending queue—not necessarily NVM—the write is considered "persistent" as they are now in the ADR (persistent) domain.

The use of cacheline flush instructions constitute a major overhead in NVM software and reducing unnecessary flushes has been a major goal in recent research. Later generations of Optane PMem (e.g., the 200 series [25]) feature extended ADR (eADR) which includes the entire CPU cache in the ADR domain (Figure 2.2), effectively providing durable CPU caches despite they are still built using traditional SRAM. The availability of eADR voids the need for software to proactively issue cacheline instructions, but the fences are still needed. In NVM index (and general NVM software) design, how to reduce the amount of cacheline flushes and fences, and leveraging eADR features are important design decisions which we will describe in later chapters.

Software Support

With the aforementioned hardware support, software generally needs to (1) perform normal memory access instructions as if on normal DRAM, (2) explicitly issue cacheline flush and/or fence instructions for proper persistence and ordering. In addition to plain load/store, cacheline flush and fence instructions provided by the CPU, software may continue to use other memory access instructions, such as compare-and-swap (CAS) [22]. However, care must be taken to ensure correctness around these memory access instructions as they only guarantee atomicity on 8-byte memory words, yet index implementations will often require atomically changing multiple 8-byte words in NVM and/or DRAM. All these require support from the OS and runtime libraries. To allow software to directly use memory instructions to access NVM, the hardware exposes memory address range information (such as the physical address range belonging to NVM vs. DRAM) to the OS. The OS then needs to provide APIs that allow mapping the physical NVM addresses to software processes' virtual address space. This process is similar to how physical–virtual memory address translation is done for normal DRAM, except that NVM is persistent, therefore also requiring an approach to recovery.

There have been numerous approaches to enable NVM programming and NVM data access, but the de facto standard is set by the Intel Persistent Memory Development Kit (PMDK) [23]. Briefly, PMDK models NVM space as "pools" that are represented by (virtual) files whose data is in fact in NVM. Access to NVM data is then enabled through memory-mapped files (through the POSIX mmap system call). NVM applications can then leverage normal file concepts to manage persistent NVM pools, while still being able to use normal memory instructions to access data because the "file" is directly mmap'ed to its address space. This is facilitated by the DAX feature provided by modern OSes, including GNU/Linux.

With NVM memory-mapped to the address space, building NVM software then further requires a programming library that can provide support for two important issues: (1) NVM management and (2) data persistence and recovery. For NVM management, the application would need a persistent allocator that can avoid permanent memory leaks. This is beyond the capabilities of traditional memory allocators for DRAM (e.g., malloc) because they cannot reliably track the ownership of a memory block upon failures—after all, all DRAM content is lost upon power cycles or restart after a crash. NVM-based software, however, must take this into account. Consider a scenario where a crash happens, yet the allocated memory is not passed to the application but is already allocated from the allocator. Upon restart, neither the application nor the allocator "thinks" it owns the memory, causing permanent memory leaks. Multiple allocators have been proposed to solve this issue; we refer interested readers to related work [8, 9, 23, 38] for more details. PMDK itself also comes with an allocator, which has been used extensively in Optane-Era NVM indexes.

For data persistence and recovery, the difficulty is often on how to ensure updates that involve writing more than eight bytes can be atomically applied. For example, consider a B+-tree split case where the splitting thread needs to modify insert into the parent node a new separator key, and redistribute keys of in one leaf node between two new leaf nodes. These operations should conceptually happen atomically, otherwise the tree will be left in an inconsistent state, e.g., with the keys redistributed but missing a pointer to the new leaf node at the parent level, effectively missing data. There are multiple notable research proposals [11, 46, 48] to handle these issues. PMDK also builds on top of prior research to provide a set of libraries. A common solution to this problem is to borrow the transactions and write-ahead logging techniques from the database systems literature. The idea is to record changes belonging to a persistent log that is located in NVM and replay then upon crash recovery. Note that here "transaction" usually refers to persistence and only guarantees to atomically persisting a set of NVM writes, instead of providing concurrency isolation. Therefore, software still needs to employ synchronization primitives and concurrency control schemes for correct multi-threading. For example, spinlocks and mutexes can still be used, but should usually be reset to an unlocked state upon recovery.

A final issue is the conversion between virtual memory pointers and NVM addresses: after an NVM pool is memory mapped into the address space of a process, the application logic uses virtual memory pointers to manipulate data and these pointer addresses may be persisted as part of the data structure. For example, an inner node in a B+-tree may need to point to its child nodes in the next level. In traditional in-memory B+-trees, the nodes will directly store virtual memory pointers. However, for NVM-based B+-trees, storing the virtual memory pointers may lead to incorrect execution after recovery, because it is not guaranteed that the same virtual address space range will be assigned across restarts. The solution usually is to store offsets of the pointed NVM blocks into the NVM pool, instead of pointers. Although this would add a translation overhead during runtime, it is negligible in practice.

References

[1] Micron announces availability of phase change memory for mobile devices (2012). URL https://investors.micron.com/news-releases/news-release-details/micron-announces-availability-phase-change-memory-mobile-devices

[2] HPE demonstrates worlds first memory-driven computing architecture (2016). URL https://www.hpe.com/us/en/newsroom/press-release/2017/03/hewlett-packard-enterprise-demonstrates-worlds-first-memory-driven-computing-architecture.html

[3] Compute Express Link™: The breakthrough cpu-to-device interconnect (2023). URL https://www.computeexpresslink.org/

[4] Future non-volatile memory systems – enhancing storage performance and reliability (2023). URL https://www.zurich.ibm.com/pcm/

[5] AgigaTech: Non-Volatile RAM (2022). URL http://www.agigatech.com. Last accessed: June 7, 2022

[6] Arulraj, J., Levandoski, J.J., Minhas, U.F., Larson, P.: BzTree: A High-Performance Latch-free Range Index for Non-Volatile Memory. PVLDB **11**(5), 553–565 (2018)

[7] Bez, R.: Chalcogenide PCM: a memory technology for next decade. In: 2009 IEEE International Electron Devices Meeting (IEDM), pp. 1–4 (2009)

[8] Bhandari, K., Chakrabarti, D.R., Boehm, H.J.: Makalu: Fast Recoverable Allocation of Non-Volatile Memory. In: Proceedings of the 2016 ACM SIGPLAN International Conference on Object-Oriented Programming, Systems, Languages, and Applications, OOPSLA 2016, p. 677–694 (2016)

[9] Cai, W., Wen, H., Beadle, H.A., Kjellqvist, C., Hedayati, M., Scott, M.L.: Understanding and Optimizing Persistent Memory Allocation. In: Proceedings of the 2020 ACM SIGPLAN International Symposium on Memory Management, ISMM 2020, p. 60–73 (2020)

[10] Chakrabarti, D.R., Boehm, H.J., Bhandari, K.: Atlas: Leveraging Locks for Non-Volatile Memory Consistency. In: Proceedings of the 2014 ACM International Conference on Object Oriented Programming Systems Languages and Applications, OOPSLA '14, p. 433–452. Association for Computing Machinery, New York, NY, USA (2014)

[11] Coburn, J., Caulfield, A.M., Akel, A., Grupp, L.M., Gupta, R.K., Jhala, R., Swanson, S.: NV-Heaps: Making Persistent Objects Fast and Safe with next-Generation, Non-Volatile Memories. In: Proceedings of the Sixteenth International Conference on Architectural Support for Programming Languages and Operating Systems, ASPLOS XVI, p. 105–118. Association for Computing Machinery, New York, NY, USA (2011)

[12] Condit, J., Nightingale, E.B., Frost, C., Ipek, E., Lee, B., Burger, D., Coetzee, D.: Better I/O through Byte-Addressable, Persistent Memory. In: Proceedings of the ACM SIGOPS 22nd Symposium on Operating Systems Principles, SOSP '09, p. 133–146 (2009)

[13] Crooke, R., Durcan, M.: A revolutionary breakthrough in memory technology. 3D XPoint Launch Keynote (2015)

[14] Everspin: (2023). URL https://www.everspin.com/spin-transfer-torque-mram-technology

[15] Gebregiorgis, A., Bishnoi, R., Tahoori, M.B.: Spintronic Normally-off Heterogeneous System-on-Chip Design. In: 2018 Design, Automation & Test in Europe Conference & Exhibition (DATE), pp. 113–118 (2018)

[16] Gervasi, B.: Memory class storage is permanently changing server architectures. Nantero Whitepapers (2023). URL https://www.nantero.com/wp-content/uploads/NRAM-White-Paper-4-1.pdf

[17] Gervasi, B., Ridgley, R.: NRAM Carbon Nanotube Non-Volatile Memory...Can DRAM be replaced? Nantero Whitepapers (2023). URL https://www.nantero.com/wp-content/uploads/Nantero-White-Paper-1-Updated.pdf

[18] Gugnani, S., Kashyap, A., Lu, X.: Understanding the Idiosyncrasies of Real Persistent Memory. PVLDB **14**(4), 626–639 (2020)

[19] Hewlett Packard Labs: The Machine: A new kind of computer (2023). URL https://www.hpl.hp.com/research/systems-research/themachine/

[20] Hosomi, M., Yamagishi, H., Yamamoto, T., Bessho, K., Higo, Y., Yamane, K., Yamada, H., Shoji, M., Hachino, H., Fukumoto, C., Nagao, H., Kano, H.: A novel nonvolatile memory with spin torque transfer magnetization switching: Spin-RAM pp. 459–462 (2005)

[21] Huang, K., Imai, D., Wang, T., Xie, D.: SSDs Striking Back: The Storage Jungle and Its Implications on Persistent Indexes. In: 12th Annual Conference on Innovative Data Systems Research, CIDR 2022, Chaminade, CA, USA, January 9-12, 2022, Online Proceedings (2022)

[22] Intel: Intel Architectures Software Developer's Manual (2021)

[23] Intel: Persistent Memory Development Kit (2021). URL http://pmem.io/pmdk. Last accessed: June 7, 2022

[24] Intel Corporation: Brief: Intel Optane Persistent Memory (2021). URL https://www.intel.ca/content/www/ca/en/products/docs/memory-storage/optane-persistent-memory/optane-dc-persistent-memory-brief.html

[25] Intel Corporation: Intel Optane Persistent Memory 200 series brief (2022). URL https://www.intel.ca/content/www/ca/en/products/docs/memory-storage/optane-persistent-memory/optane-persistent-memory-200-series-brief.html

[26] Izraelevitz, J., Yang, J., Zhang, L., Kim, J., Liu, X., Memaripour, A., Soh, Y.J., Wang, Z., Xu, Y., Dulloor, S.R., Zhao, J., Swanson, S.: Basic performance measurements of the Intel Optane DC Persistent Memory Module (2019)

[27] Jog, A., Mishra, A.K., Xu, C., Xie, Y., Narayanan, V., Iyer, R., Das, C.R.: Cache revive: Architecting volatile stt-ram caches for enhanced performance in cmps. In: DAC Design Automation Conference 2012, pp. 243–252 (2012)

[28] Kimura, H.: FOEDUS: OLTP Engine for a Thousand Cores and NVRAM. In: Proceedings of the 2015 ACM SIGMOD International Conference on Management of Data, SIGMOD '15, p. 691–706. Association for Computing Machinery, New York, NY, USA (2015)

[29] Lee, B.C., Ipek, E., Mutlu, O., Burger, D.: Architecting Phase Change Memory as a Scalable Dram Alternative. In: Proceedings of the 36th Annual International Symposium on Computer Architecture, ISCA '09, p. 2–13. Association for Computing Machinery, New York, NY, USA (2009)

[30] Lersch, L., Hao, X., Oukid, I., Wang, T., Willhalm, T.: Evaluating Persistent Memory Range Indexes. PVLDB 13(4), 574–587 (2019)

[31] Mellor, C.: Is Optane DIMM endurance good enough? Quick answer... Yes, Intel has delivered (2019). URL https://blocksandfiles.com/2019/04/04/enduring-optane-dimm-question-is-its-endurance-good-enough-yes-intel-has-delivered/

[32] Microsoft: Transaction Commit latency acceleration using Storage Class Memory in Windows Server 2016/SQL Server 2016 SP1 (2016). URL https://learn.microsoft.com/en-ca/archive/blogs/sqlserverstorageengine/transaction-commit-latency-acceleration-using-storage-class-memory-in-windows-server-2016sql-server-2016-sp1

[33] Morgan, T.P.: Finally, a coherent interconnect strategy: CXL absorbs Gen-Z (2021). URL https://www.nextplatform.com/2021/11/23/finally-a-coherent-interconnect-strategy-cxl-absorbs-gen-z/

[34] Nantero: Explore our technology ecosystem – Advancements in Nanotechnology (2023). URL https://www.nantero.com/technology/

[35] Qureshi, M.K., Karidis, J., Franceschini, M., Srinivasan, V., Lastras, L., Abali, B.: Enhancing Lifetime and Security of PCM-Based Main Memory with Start-Gap Wear Leveling. In: Proceedings of the 42nd Annual IEEE/ACM International Symposium on Microarchitecture, MICRO 42, p. 14–23 (2009)

[36] van Renen, A., Vogel, L., Leis, V., Neumann, T., Kemper, A.: Persistent memory I/O primitives. In: Proceedings of the 15th International Workshop on Data Management on New Hardware, DaMoN 2019., pp. 12:1–12:7 (2019)

[37] Rudoff, A.: Deprecating the PCOMMIT instruction (2016). URL https://software.intel.com/en-us/blogs/2016/09/12/deprecate-pcommit-instruction

[38] Schwalb, D., Berning, T., Faust, M., Dreseler, M., Plattner, H.: nvm malloc: Memory allocation for nvram. In: R. Bordawekar, T. Lahiri, B. Gedik, C.A. Lang (eds.) ADMS@VLDB, pp. 61–72 (2015). URL http://dblp.uni-trier.de/db/conf/vldb/adms2015.html#SchwalbBFDP15

[39] Secco, J., Corinto, F., Sebastian, A.: Flux-Charge Memristor Model for Phase Change Memory. IEEE Trans. Circuits Syst. II Express Briefs 65-II(1), 111–114 (2018)

[40] Song, S., Das, A., Mutlu, O., Kandasamy, N.: Improving Phase Change Memory Performance with Data Content Aware Access. In: Proceedings of the 2020

ACM SIGPLAN International Symposium on Memory Management, ISMM 2020, p. 30–47 (2020)

[41] Strukov, D.B., Snider, G.S., Stewart, D.R., Williams, R.S.: The missing memristor found. Nature **453**(7191), 80–83 (2008)

[42] Sun, Z., Bi, X., Li, H., Wong, W.F., Ong, Z.L., Zhu, X., Wu, W.: Multi retention level stt-ram cache designs with a dynamic refresh scheme. In: 2011 44th Annual IEEE/ACM International Symposium on Microarchitecture (MICRO), pp. 329–338 (2011)

[43] Verheyde, A.: Intel demonstrates STT-MRAM for L4 cache (2019). URL https://www.tomshardware.com/news/intel-demonstrates-stt-mram-for-l4-cache

[44] Viking Technology: NVDIMM - Fastest Tier in Your Storage Strategy (2014). URL https://snia.org/sites/default/files/NVDIMM\%20FastestTier_0.pdf

[45] Viking Technology: DDR4 NVDIMM (2017). Retrieved August 17, 2021 from http://www.vikingtechnology.com

[46] Volos, H., Tack, A.J., Swift, M.M.: Mnemosyne: Lightweight Persistent Memory. In: Proceedings of the Sixteenth International Conference on Architectural Support for Programming Languages and Operating Systems, ASPLOS XVI, p. 91–104. Association for Computing Machinery, New York, NY, USA (2011)

[47] Wang, T., Johnson, R.: Scalable Logging through Emerging Non-Volatile Memory. PVLDB **7**(10), 865–876 (2014)

[48] Wang, T., Levandoski, J., Larson, P.A.: Easy lock-free indexing in non-volatile memory. In: 2018 IEEE 34th International Conference on Data Engineering (ICDE), pp. 461–472 (2018)

[49] Wong, H.S.P., Raoux, S., Kim, S., Liang, J., Reifenberg, J.P., Rajendran, B., Asheghi, M., Goodson, K.E.: Phase change memory. Proceedings of the IEEE **98**(12), 2201–2227 (2010)

[50] Yang, J., Kim, J., Hoseinzadeh, M., Izraelevitz, J., Swanson, S.: An Empirical Guide to the Behavior and Use of Scalable Persistent Memory. In: Proceedings of the 18th USENIX Conference on File and Storage Technologies, FAST'20, p. 169–182 (2020)

[51] Zhou, P., Zhao, B., Yang, J., Zhang, Y.: A Durable and Energy Efficient Main Memory Using Phase Change Memory Technology. In: Proceedings of the 36th Annual International Symposium on Computer Architecture, ISCA '09, p. 14–23. Association for Computing Machinery, New York, NY, USA (2009)

Chapter 3
A Primer on Database Indexing

Abstract This chapter introduces the basics of indexing for OLTP databases. We will start with the overall concept of indexing and discuss indexes commonly used by OLTP systems, in particular trees and hash tables. Readers already familiar with these topics may skim and fast forward to later chapters.

3.1 Overview

An index by definition maps keys to values. Through such mappings, an index can provide fast data access by looking up keys, instead of full table scans. In the context of relational databases, an index typically is built on one or multiple columns with column values (i.e., the record field corresponding to the columns) as keys, and "data entries" as values. There are three alternative types of data entries [12]: (1) an actual table record, (2) the address or a record ID (RID), or (3) a list of RIDs. Alternative 1 in fact is a special table storage format as it contains actual table data, while Alternatives 2 and 3 separate the table and its indexes by providing a way to locate the desired record(s).

Indexes must be kept consistent with the underlying table. When table records are updated, the corresponding index that use the updated fields as keys (and values if Alternative 1 is used) must also be updated. Key updates can be done by providing explicit support by the index or by deleting the old key and inserting the new key. Inserting/deleting a record to the underlying table also means an insert/delete operation needs to be issued to the associated indexes. How to keep the index and table consistent is an important problem but out of the scope of this book.

There have been numerous index structures, however, they can all be categorized by whether range scan is supported. Range indexes, such as various tree structures and tries, support both point queries (insert, delete, update and lookup) and range queries that return a set values of a range of keys (specified by a start key and an end key or the number of keys followed by the start key). The rest of this chapter gives an overview of classic designs of both types of indexes, which are used as baselines

K. Huang, T. Wang, *Indexing on Non-Volatile Memory*, SpringerBriefs in Computer Science,
https://doi.org/10.1007/978-3-031-47627-3_3

for more recent NVM indexes discussed in later chapters. For each index, we discuss their structure, how they support common index operations and concurrency control.

3.2 Range Indexes

In this section, we describe two main types of range indexes: B+-trees and tries. We begin with their structures and operations, and then discuss how concurrency is typically supported.

3.2.1 B+-trees

B+-trees [1] (or simply *B-trees*[1]) are perhaps the most versatile range index that can be found in most serious database management systems implementations. Popular DBMS products—such as Microsoft SQL Server, Oracle, MySQL and PostgreSQL—all implement some variant of B+-trees.

A B+-tree consists of multiple levels of nodes, each of which is usually fixed-size, being multiples of I/O size (e.g., disk sector size or flash page size) for storage-centric designs, or multiples of cacheline sizes for in-memory designs. As we will see later, for NVM designs, node size is further usually aligned to NVM's internal access granularity (e.g., 256-byte for Optane PMem). Higher level nodes guide search traffic and only the leaf nodes at the lowest level store actual data entries using one of the previously mentioned three alternatives.

The tree starts with an empty "root" node and gradually grows as more keys are inserted. To insert a key-value pair, the inserting thread first traverses down the tree to locate the target leaf node. It then checks whether the node still has enough space to accommodate the new key-value pair, and if so, the key and data entry are inserted to the node. Note that usually keys are sorted in each node to allow binary search and provide better search performance during lookups. However, if there is not enough space in the leaf node, a split operation needs to be performed to split the target leaf node into two, and generate a new separator key that is inserted to the parent node of the original target leaf node. As a result, the parent node could subsequently need to be split, so are the upper level nodes until the root node, eventually causing the tree to grow. Conversely, a delete operation may cause leaf nodes and subsequently higher level nodes to be merged with siblings, eventually causing the tree to shrink.

---

[1] Both "B+-trees' and "B-tree" refer to B+-trees in database literature [12].

3.2.2 Radix Trees (Tries)

Unlike B-trees that compare full keys at different levels to guide search, radix trees directly use the key bytes to guide key lookups. Conceptually, each node in the next level represents the next character of the key until the key word is exhausted. This means the maximum tree height is bounded by the longest key length, instead of by the number of key-value pairs (records) being indexed, which can be very attractive for large data sets. However, when the key space is sparse, tries can occupy much more space than other indexes such as B-trees.

There have been various proposals to mitigate this issue [2, 7]. A classic example in this space is the adaptive radix tree (ART) [7], which was taken as the baseline for most trie-based indexes for NVM.

The key ideas of ART is to use adaptive node sizes, in addition to techniques such as path compression and lazy expansion to allow high space efficiency and high performance. As shown in Figure 3.1, instead of resizing nodes after every update, which can be expensive, ART proposes four inner node types, including Node4, Node16, Node 48 and Node256, depending on the maximum capacity of the node. As the name suggests, a Node4 node can store up to four (sorted) partial keys and up to four pointers to child nodes. Node16 is the same as Node4, except that it stores up to 16 partial keys and up to 16 child pointers. Therefore, Node16 is used when the number of keys is between 5 and 16. The other two types are Node48 and Node256. If a node has between 17 and 48 child pointers, ART uses a child index array to map partial keys to child pointers, which is more space-efficient than storing 256 8-byte pointers. Node256 is used when a node has more than 48 child pointers and can store no more than 256 child pointers, one for each possible key byte.

Data entries (values) in ART can be stored in three different ways. The first is single-value leaves where each node stores a single value, allowing keys and values of different lengths within a tree. The downside is that an extra pointer chasing is needed to access the value. The second approach is multi-value leaves which use the same structures of inner nodes, but stores values instead of pointers. As a result, all the keys in the tree should have the same length to use this approach. The third approach combines pointers and values in slots, taking the best of both of the aforementioned two approaches. Each pointer in an inner node can store either a pointer or a value, differentiated by an extra bit in the pointer (e.g., the most significant bit).

As mentioned, a drawback of tries is that long keys and skewed key distributions can lead to very long branches (deeper trie) that can lower lookup performance. ART further uses lazy expansion and path compression to efficiently index long keys. The former allows inner nodes to be created only when they are needed to distinguish at least two leaf nodes, and the latter eliminates single-child inner node paths. These techniques allow skipping unnecessary extra levels and thus reducing the tree depth and improving performance.

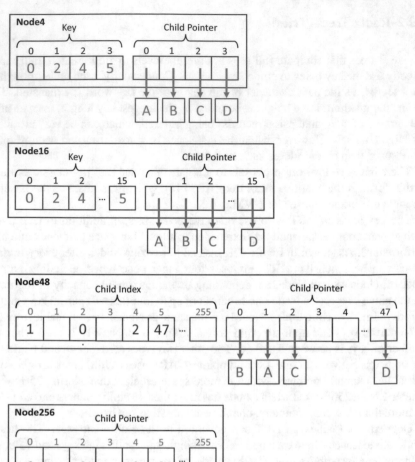

Fig. 3.1: Inner node types in ART.

3.3 Hash Tables

An effective hash table implementation consists of two components: a hashing scheme and a hash function. The hashing scheme manages key collisions that may occur during the hashing process, and the hash function maps a large key space into a smaller domain. While the selection of an appropriate hash function is crucial, it is the hashing scheme that plays a vital role in the design of hash tables to suit different architecture. Therefore, we will focus on revisiting several well-established hashing schemes. Generally, a hashing scheme can be static or dynamic. The former does

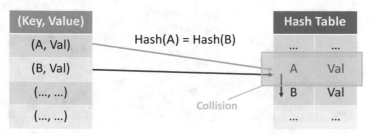

Fig. 3.2: An example of hash collision and linear probing where both keys A and B are hashed to the same bucket.

not allow growing/shrinking as the data size grows/shrinks. A full-table rehashing is required to do so; this rehashing process is often blocking, leading to service downtime. The latter can gracefully grow/shrink during runtime as the data size changes without service downtime. Below we start with static hashing, and then build on top of it to introduce dynamic hashing.

3.3.1 Static Hashing

As its name suggests, static hashing fixes the size of the hash table which consists of buckets, each of which in turn can store multiple key-value pairs (data entries). That is, the number of buckets is determined upon creation and remains constant throughout the lifetime of the data structure. The advantage of a static hashing scheme is its simplicity and predictable performance. Since the size (i.e., number of buckets) of the hash table is predetermined, it is easier to allocate memory and calculate the hash function. However, one limitation is that if the number of elements to be stored exceeds the capacity of the hash table, it may result in increased collisions, reduced performance, and the need to rebuild the hash table. When a collision occurs in a static hashing scheme, various techniques such as linear probing or cuckoo hashing can be used to resolve the collisions. These techniques allow for efficient storage and retrieval of data even when collisions occur.

Linear Probing. When a collision occurs, we perform a linear search through adjacent buckets/slots until we find an open one. For instance, consider the scenario in Figure 3.2, where both key A and key B are mapped to the same bucket in the hash table. When we attempt to insert key B, we discover that key A has already occupied that bucket. Consequently, we conduct a linear search to find the next available bucket where we can insert key B. During lookups, we can determine the bucket where the desired key hashes to and then linearly search through the table until we find the desired entry, if it exists. However, it is worth noting that when the hash table becomes full, a more extensive process is required. In such cases, we need to rebuild the entire hash table using larger tables to accommodate additional entries.

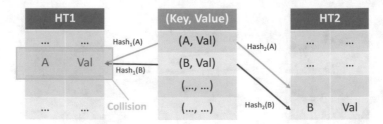

Fig. 3.3: Cuckoo hashing where two tables along with two hash functions are used to determine the better placement of a record upon collision.

Cuckoo Hashing. As an alternative to using a single hash table, cuckoo hashing [11] employs multiple hash tables with different hash functions. This approach is sketched in Figure 3.3. During insertion, each table is examined to identify a free slot. If multiple tables have available slots, factors like load factor can be compared, or a random table can be selected. In the event that no table has a free slot, a random table is chosen and an existing entry is evicted. The evicted entry is then rehashed and placed into a different table. Occasionally, there may be cases where a cycle is formed, necessitating the rebuilding of the hash table using larger tables. Additionally, when the tables reach their maximum capacity, a complete rebuilding of the hash tables becomes necessary.

3.3.2 Dynamic Hashing

A dynamic hashing scheme differs from a static hashing scheme in its ability to adjust the number of hash buckets dynamically as the number of elements changes. Unlike a static scheme that necessitates rebuilding the entire hash table when it reaches full capacity to accommodate additional elements, a dynamic hashing scheme offers the flexibility to adapt the table's size in real-time. Two classic approaches to dynamic hashing are extendible hashing and linear hashing, which we introduce next.

Extendible Hashing

The key idea of extendible hashing is to allow buckets to be created and deleted on demand and track these buckets in another array called the directory. Each entry in the directory records the location (e.g., using 8 bytes) of a bucket. Since the directory is very small, it can be easily reallocated and dynamically adjusted as the number of buckets grow or reduce. For this to work, extendible hashing maintains two parameters: the global depth and local depth. The global depth indicates how many bits of the hash value we need to compare in order to find the corresponding bucket. We can compare the most significant bit or the least significant bit. The local

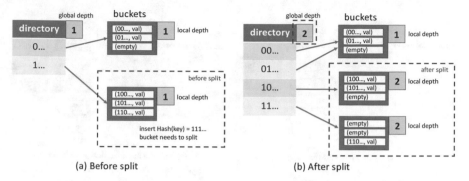

(a) Before split   (b) After split

Fig. 3.4: Extendible hashing. A global directory indexes all the buckets which are created and deleted on demand. Each bucket may store multiple records and can be split after it is full. Each directory entry points to a bucket and upon bucket split, the directory is doubled if there is no free entry. Otherwise, the address of the new bucket is added to the corresponding slot in the directory. This is determined by the local and global depths parameters.

depth is maintained per bucket and indicates whether we need to double the size of the directory when we split the bucket. Specifically, if the local depth is not less than the global depth, we need to expand the directory.

Figure 3.4 illustrates an example of how extendible hashing resizes the hash table. When we insert a key whose hash value starts with three consecutive 1s, we check the directory and determine that any value starting with 1 should be directed to this bucket, which needs to be split. Since the local depth is equal to the global depth, we double the size of the directory so that we can compare more bits before accessing the bucket. After the split, we can observe that the bucket at the top remains unchanged, and its local depth remains 1. In the future, if we want to split this bucket again, we don't need to expand the directory because there are now two pointers pointing to the same bucket. One of these pointers can be used to point to the new bucket. Overall, we can conclude that expanding the directory is a lighter operation compared to rebuilding the entire table.

3.3.2.1 Linear Hashing

The need to double the directory size upon bucket splitting is inevitable in extendible hashing. However, can we develop a growth strategy that is smoother and more seamless? The answer is indeed affirmative. Linear hashing [5, 10] offers a remedy to the maintenance and memory burdens imposed by the manipulation of the global directory by localizing the split process. With linear hashing, when an overflow occurs, the targeted bucket for splitting is always the one currently being looked at the split pointer, regardless of whether it is the exact bucket that needs to overflow. Similar to the concept of cuckoo hashing, linear hashing leverages multiple hash

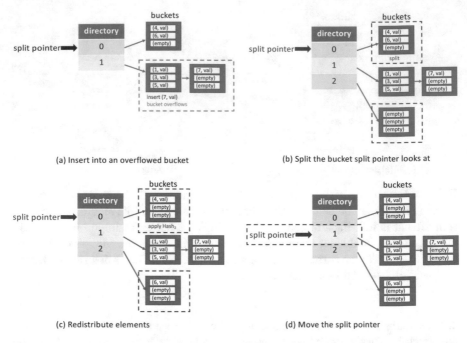

(a) Insert into an overflowed bucket   (b) Split the bucket split pointer looks at

(c) Redistribute elements   (d) Move the split pointer

Fig. 3.5: Linear hashing. The bucket to be split is not necessarily the bucket that is full. The original design of linear hashing avoids the use of a directory, but recent practical implementations (including NVM-based ones) often still use a directory to easily track buckets allocated in volatile DRAM memory or NVM.

functions, which allows for the redistribution of data items amongst the newly created buckets. This redistribution not only balances load but also facilitates efficient data retrieval. After each split, the split pointer moves to the subsequent bucket in a cyclic manner. Therefore, eventually each bucket has an even chance of being split.

Figure 3.5 shows an example of how linear hashing expands the hash table. The hash table initially uses $Hash_1(key) = key \; mod \; n$ to distribute elements. Here, we have n = 2. When we want to insert an element with a key of 7, a bucket will overflow. As the first step (a), we create a new bucket linked to the overflowed bucket to accommodate (7, val). In (b), we check the split pointer to split the bucket it is looking at and add a new directory to point to the newly created bucket. In (c), we apply another hash function, $Hash_2(key) = key \; mod \; 2n$, to every single element in the bucket that directory 0 points to. Here, the element with a key of 6 gets redistributed to the new bucket, because its hash value is 6 mod 4 = 2. Finally, we move the split pointer to the next slot in the directory.

3.4 Index Concurrency Control

When multiple threads need to access a B-tree index, it is important to ensure threads see consistent data, especially when updates and SMOs are involved. The classic approach to supporting concurrency for B-trees is latch coupling[2]: each tree node is associated with a latch which can be a mutex, spinlock, or other synchronization primitive that allow reader-writer modes. Whenever a node is accessed, the thread will acquire the latch protecting the node in the corresponding mode (either reader or writer). As the traversal continues from the root to leaf levels, the thread keeps acquiring latches, at each level, but will release the previous level latches once it is clear that even an SMO at the lower level will not cause the current level to be split. This way, usually a thread only needs to hold at most two latches at the same time.

The original latch coupling approach is usually pessimistic by requiring readers to also acquire the lock, causing shared memory writes even for read-only workloads. Some systems then use optimistic lock coupling [6], which was also adopted by in-memory trie indexes [8] as we describe later. The basic idea is to use versioned latches, instead of traditional reader-writer locks in the aforementioned latch coupling protocol. As a result, readers do not need to issue synchronization instructions such as CAS during traversal, but only need to verify that the node content read is consistent by verifying the version associated with the node (which is typically part of the latch itself) has not changed. Only the writer needs to issue synchronization instructions to acquire the lock in exclusive mode. This way, read-only or read-mostly workloads can proceed with very low overhead as little shared-memory writes were issued. The drawback, however, is that such optimistic locks are inherently writer-biased, because a reader is destined to fail if a concurrent writer started during the read operation. Some recent approaches have proposed solutions to solve this problem by combining pessimistic reader modes [3].

An important issue with latch-based concurrency is that a thread may hold the latch for an indefinite amount of time, blocking overall progress. Some indexes introduces lock-free approaches to B-tree concurrency. Lock-free algorithms guarantees system overall progress by allowing threads to inspect each other's internal state and thus "help-along" each other to avoid blocking progress. These algorithms directly use hardware-provided synchronization primitives (e.g., CAS), which can only atomically change memory word of limited widths, e.g., 8-byte. Therefore, the difficulty lies in how to ensure correct synchronization when multiple 8-byte words need to be modified atomically. B-tree operations can often involve such cases. For example, when a split is necessary, the thread needs to atomically modify multiple pointer, e.g., to change the pointers in the parent node to point to the new leaf nodes and inserting a new separator key to the parent node. The BwTree [9] is a classic example of lock-free concurrency for B-trees and solves the aforementioned prob-

---

[2] Also known as "lock coupling." In database literature, synchronization primitives used for physical layer data structures, such as indexes, are called "latches" whereas the term "lock" is for logical level concurrency control. Latches are usually what are called "locks" in OS literature and can be mutex, spinlocks, etc. Since our focus is physical level data structure (i.e., indexes), when the context is clear we use the two terms interchangeably.

lem by using logical node IDs, instead of virtual memory pointers, in tree nodes. It then uses a "mapping table to map logical node IDs to physical pointers, saving certain pointer changing operations in tree nodes. The downside is that each node access now requires indirection through the mapping table, in addition to increased implementation complexity.

Most recent indexes (including in-memory and NVM-based) use optimistic approaches because they offer good performance and are easier to implement and debug than lock-free approaches. Other approaches, such as hardware transactional memory (HTM) have also seen adoption in NVM-based indexes. We describe these approaches and their adaptations in NVM indexes in later chapters. For a more comprehensive discussion on index concurrency control, we refer interested readers to other survey articles for details [4].

References

[1] Bayer, R., McCreight, E.: Organization and Maintenance of Large Ordered Indices. In: Proceedings of the 1970 ACM SIGFIDET (Now SIGMOD) Workshop on Data Description, Access and Control, SIGFIDET '70, p. 107–141. Association for Computing Machinery, New York, NY, USA (1970)

[2] Binna, R., Zangerle, E., Pichl, M., Specht, G., Leis, V.: HOT: A Height Optimized Trie Index for Main-Memory Database Systems. In: Proceedings of the 2018 International Conference on Management of Data, SIGMOD '18, p. 521–534 (2018)

[3] Böttcher, J., Leis, V., Giceva, J., Neumann, T., Kemper, A.: Scalable and Robust Latches for Database Systems. In: Proceedings of the 16th International Workshop on Data Management on New Hardware, DaMoN '20. Association for Computing Machinery, New York, NY, USA (2020)

[4] Graefe, G.: A Survey of B-Tree Locking Techniques. ACM Trans. Database Syst. **35**(3) (2010)

[5] Larson, P.A.: Dynamic hash tables. Commun. ACM **31**(4), 446–457 (1988)

[6] Leis, V., Haubenschild, M., Neumann, T.: Optimistic Lock Coupling: A Scalable and Efficient General-Purpose Synchronization Method. IEEE Data Eng. Bull. **42**, 73–84 (2019)

[7] Leis, V., Kemper, A., Neumann, T.: The Adaptive Radix Tree: ARTful Indexing for Main-Memory Databases. In: Proceedings of the 2013 IEEE International Conference on Data Engineering, ICDE '13, p. 38–49 (2013)

[8] Leis, V., Scheibner, F., Kemper, A., Neumann, T.: The ART of Practical Synchronization. In: Proceedings of the 12th International Workshop on Data Management on New Hardware, DaMoN '16 (2016)

[9] Levandoski, J.J., Lomet, D.B., Sengupta, S.: The Bw-Tree: A B-tree for new hardware platforms. In: Proceedings of the 2013 IEEE International Conference on Data Engineering (ICDE 2013), ICDE '13, pp. 302–313 (2013)

[10] Litwin, W.: Linear hashing: A new tool for file and table addressing. In: Proceedings of the Sixth International Conference on Very Large Data Bases - Volume 6, VLDB '80, pp. 212–223. VLDB Endowment (1980)

[11] Pagh, R., Rodler, F.F.: Cuckoo Hashing. J. Algorithms **51**(2), 122–144 (2004)

[12] Ramakrishnan, R., Gehrke, J.: Database Management Systems, 3 edn. (2003)

Chapter 4
Range Indexes on Non-Volatile Memory

Abstract In this chapter, we survey range indexes built for non-volatile memory. They are typically built on top of B+-trees, tries, or a hybrid of both. Our discussion will focus on the additional features and necessary modifications tailored for NVM on top of conventional indexes.

4.1 Introduction

With the background laid out, from this section we start to discuss actual NVM-based index designs. This chapter will cover a number of indexes on NVM that support both point and range queries (i.e., scans). Most of them are adaptations of B+-trees, which are arguably the most widely used range indexes in most (if not all) database systems, and thus received perhaps the most attention for NVM adaptation. The NVM indexes introduced in this chapter are also adaptations of DRAM baseline, i.e., in-memory B+-trees and tries. This makes it tempting for NVM-based range indexes to compare with their in-memory counterparts, and to make it an ultimate goal to match the performance of in-memory range indexes. As we go through the different proposals in the following sections, a lot of techniques were proposed based on this goal.

In the following, we start with pre-Optane range index proposals, followed by NVM range indexes proposed after Optane PMem became available. For each index, we focus on their overall structure and then expand on their unique designs for NVM. Much of the discussion in this chapter is based on prior work [7, 13] which we suggest interested readers to explore for more details (such as runtime performance behaviours of these indexes).

© The Author(s), under exclusive license to Springer Nature Switzerland AG 2024
K. Huang, T. Wang, *Indexing on Non-Volatile Memory*, SpringerBriefs in Computer Science,
https://doi.org/10.1007/978-3-031-47627-3_4

4.2 Pre-Optane NVM Range Indexes

We start with four NVM range indexes proposed before the actual hardware (Optane) became available. Perhaps coincidentally, they are all based on B+-trees. They cover a range of system design aspects and tradeoffs, such as using lock-based, lock-free and optimistic locking approaches for concurrency control, and using unsorted tree nodes and selective persistence to reduce unnecessary NVM accesses. There are more pre-Optane NVM indexes, but the designs proposed by these indexes are either representative or have greatly impacted the design of subsequent NVM indexes.

4.2.1 Write-Atomic B+-tree (wB⁺-Tree)

The wB^+-Tree [4] is one of the early B+-tree variants that optimize for NVM. It was proposed originally as a single-threaded data structure because the focus was mainly on reducing unnecessary cacheline flushes and NVM writes.

Tree Structure

wB^+-Tree is largely based on the traditional B+-tree structure, with both inner and leaf nodes in NVM. As a purely NVM-resident index, it is capable of providing instant recovery. Traditional B+-trees were designed mostly for DRAM and SSD. As we mentioned in Chapter 3, such indexes keep key-value pairs sorted in each node, in order to leverage binary search for better lookup performance. The implication of this design is that inserting a key to a node (inner or leaf) would often require shifting existing keys around to place the new key in the right position. To delete a key from a node, we also often need to shift the subsequent keys to avoid leaving a "hole" in the middle of the node. It turns out that without care, keeping NVM-resident tree nodes sorted can cause both correctness and performance issues. (1) Moving keys involves reading and writing more than 8 bytes of data in the node, which is beyond the atomic unit for NVM reads and writes. A crash during the shift could then leave the tree in an inconsistent state. Figure 4.1(a) shows an example. (2) NVM has both limited write endurance (at least assumed so when wB^+-Tree was proposed) and lower-than-DRAM write performance, so frequently moving keys will lower both NVM lifetime and performance. wB^+-Tree features two important solutions (unsorted nodes and indirection) that departed from traditional B+-tree designs. Both techniques are also often used by NVM indexes proposed after wB^+-Tree. We discuss them next.

Unsorted Nodes

Since keeping nodes sorted can cause various issues, a very straightforward yet effective solutions is to loosen this requirement and use unsorted nodes. This has

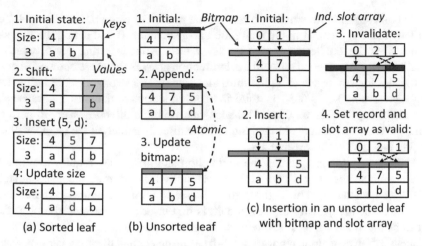

Fig. 4.1: Node structure designs for NVM-based B+-trees. wB+-Tree adopts unsorted nodes (b) and employs indirection to support binary search and more efficient range queries (c). Taken from [13], published under CC BY-NC-ND 4.0, reprinted with permission.

been proposed by earlier work [3] and is adopted by wB+-Tree. Figures 4.1(b–c) describe the idea. As shown by Figure 4.1(b), a node consists of a number of slots, each of which can store a key-value pair. The validity of slots (i.e., whether a slot contains a valid record or free) is indicated by a bitmap (the green and red boxes in the figure, respectively representing valid and free slots). To insert a record, the key-value pair is first appended at the end of the slots, and then the corresponding bit in the bitmap is updated. Since the bitmap is compact (one bit per slot), it can be updated using 8-byte atomic writes. Note that the ordering here is important: the data must be written before the validity bitmap is updated. Otherwise, a crash may leave the tree in an inconsistent state with the bitmap indicating "valid" slots that contain partial data.

Using unsorted nodes naturally avoids shifting data, but also requires linear search of the slots to find a target record and may require a separate sorting pass for scan operations which cannot simply return after scanning the requested number records following the start key. These factors can reduce performance, so the true effectiveness of using unsorted nodes also depends on the relative overheads brought by such tradeoffs. wB+-Tree solves these problems by employing indirection.

Indirection

In addition to the bitmap, wB+-Tree also maintains an indirection slot array in each node. As shown in Figure 4.1(c), an entry in the indirection slot array record the address of the actual record slot in sorted order. That is, the n-th indirection slot array entry points to the n-th smallest record in the node. For example, in Figure 4.1(c), initially the first element in the indirection array contains 0, indicating the first slot (index 0) is the smallest, followed by key 7 next. After inserting key 5, which is smaller than 7, the second entry in the indirection array is therefore updated to point to the slot for key 5, which is the third slot (index 2). Meanwhile, the indirection slot representing key 7 (i.e., the third indirection slot) is updated to 1 because slot 1 contains key 7. This way, point lookups can use the indirection array to perform binary search, and scan operations can use it to directly gather all the results without having to use an extra sorting pass.

Unlike the bitmap, updating the indirection slot array may require multiple 8-byte atomic writes. A crash could then potentially leave it in an inconsistent state. wB⁺-Tree dedicates one bit in the bitmap (left-most bit in the figure) to indicate the validity of the array. After the new record is first inserted to the slot, the bit is first set to be invalid and then is set to be valid after all the updates are done. If a crash happens in between, upon recovery wB⁺-Tree can detect that the array is inconsistent and rebuild it.

4.2.2 NV-Tree

NV-Tree [20] is also a single-threaded B+-tree-based design that is fully NVM-resident. It proposes selective consistency to further reduce the amount of NVM accesses needed during tree operations.

Tree Structure

To optimize for performance, NV-Tree makes two structural changes based on traditional B+-trees. The first change is to use unsorted nodes, while the second change is to places inner nodes in contiguous (non-volatile) memory (thus replacing pointers with offsets), as shown in Figure 4.2(top).

Like we have discussed for wB⁺-Tree, using unsorted nodes allows NV-Tree to avoid shifting keys during inserts and deletes. NV-Tree also uses an append-only strategy to accommodate node modifications. As Figure 4.2(bottom) shows, for insert, the record is directly appended at the end of the node with a positive flag. The record counter (at the beginning of the node) is then incremented to reflect the addition of a key. Note that in this process, NV-Tree does not check whether the key already exists (which is typically done for traditional B+-trees). This means the lookup logic will need to change: to search for a key in a node, NV-Tree scans the node backwards and returns the current record if its key matches the target *and* its flag is toggled to positive.

The purpose of placing all inner nodes in contiguous NVM is to obtain better hit rates and space utilization for the CPU cache. The tradeoff, however, is that upon split, the inner node layer may need to be rebuilt if new nodes need to be added.

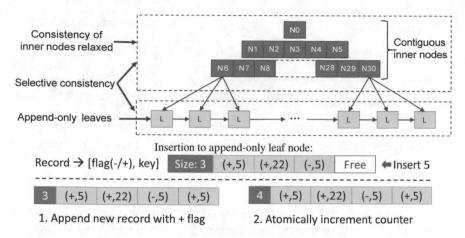

Fig. 4.2: NV-Tree architecture (top) and insertion process (bottom). Taken from [13], published under CC BY-NC-ND 4.0, reprinted with permission.

NV-Tree mitigates this cost by rebuilding the inner nodes sparsely, at the cost of higher memory footprint.

Selective Consistency

The key observation made by NV-Tree is that the B+-tree inner nodes are reconstructible from leaf nodes, making it possible to loosen the consistency requirements of inner nodes. For example, proactive cacheline flushes after modifications are done to inner nodes can be skipped. Consistency for leaf nodes is still enforced via cacheline flushes and atomic NVM writes. This can significantly save cacheline flushes and NVM accesses, thus improving performance. The downside is that since consistency is not guaranteed for inner nodes must be rebuilt upon restart based on the (consistent) leaf nodes. Although NV-Tree was originally fully NVM-resident, we note that in fact its inner nodes can be placed in DRAM to obtain even better performance given the inner nodes are not kept consistent in NVM. Additionally, the tree can be checkpointed to avoid such rebuilds upon clean shut down.

4.2.3 Fingerprinting B+-tree (FPTree)

The Fingerprinting B+-tree (FPTree) [18] also optimizes for NVM by avoiding unnecessary NVM accesses. It does so by several techniques, two of which are unique and has been followed by many subsequent designs. The first design proposes to place inner nodes in DRAM, and the second design adds "fingerprints" of keys which can allow (negative) searches to return early. FPTree was also one of the first

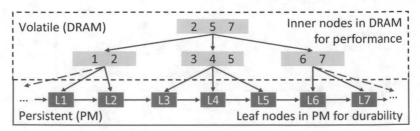

Fig. 4.3: Overview of FPTree. Taken from [13], published under CC BY-NC-ND 4.0, reprinted with permission.

NVM-based indexes that take concurrency control into consideration, by using a combination of hardware transactional memory (HTM) and traditional locking. We describe these techniques in detail below.

Tree Structure

In addition to using unsorted leaf nodes, FPTree leverages DRAM to help accelerate index operations while maintaining data persistence. It makes a similar observation to NV-Tree's: the inner nodes of a B+-tree can be reconstructed using leaf nodes. Therefore, there is not only no need to keep them consistent (like what NV-Tree does), but also no need to even use NVM to store them, eliminating the need for NVM accesses on inner nodes altogether. As shown Figure 4.3, inner nodes in FPTree are placed in DRAM, while the leaf nodes are placed on NVM. The obvious tradeoff again is that the inner nodes need to be rebuilt upon recovery. FPTree thus trades recovery time for runtime performance.

Fingerprinting

Using unsorted leaf nodes and placing inner nodes in DRAM can reduce a large amount of NVM accesses. But searching through leaf nodes remains expensive, especially under concurrent execution where node-level locking is involved. To further reduce NVM accesses at the leaf level, FPTree introduces "fingerprints" in leaf nodes. Fingerprints are single-byte hashes of keys that indicate whether the keys possibly exist in the node. They are placed contiguously at the beginning of each node (i.e., the first cacheline) for better locality. To search for a key, the execution thread first generates its fingerprint by hashing the key and taking the first byte. It then tries to find matching fingerprints (instead of actual keys) by searching through the fingerprint array. The actual records are only searched only if there is a match. Otherwise, if a fingerprint is absent for the target key, then it is guaranteed that the key is not in the node, allowing the search to terminate early and thus saving unnecessary NVM accesses. As we we will see later, fingerprinting is adopted by many subsequent trees beyond (e.g., hash tables on NVM) because of its effectiveness in accelerating lookup operations (which are also the basis insert/update/delete operations because they need to first check for key existence or find the target key).

Selective Concurrency

Prior proposals such as NV-Tree and wB$^+$-Tree are usually single-threaded and/or adopt traditional pessimistic lock coupling which can cause high overhead when the index is in-memory (DRAM or NVM). Based on the DRAM-NVM structure, FPTree also uses different concurrency control algorithms for the inner and leaf nodes. For the former, it employs hardware transactional memory (HTM) which is available on most Intel x86 CPUs. HTM provides both fast performance and easy programming paradigm, where the index developer only needs to specify single-threaded logic wrapped as transactions. The underlying cache coherence protocol then transparently detects conflicts and ensures correct transaction isolation among threads. However, its current implementation is quite limited, for example, by limiting the footprint size of the transaction to CPU L1 cache size. Moreover, a software-based fallback path that is essentially a global lock is needed in case transactions keep failing. HTM also disallows cacheline flush instructions inside the transaction as they will cause transactions to abort, FPTree therefore uses fine-grained leaf-level locking for leaf nodes.

4.2.4 BzTree

Different from the proposals we have discussed so far, BzTree [1] how B+-trees can be built as lock-free data structures on NVM with lower programming complexity. It employs a persistent multiword compare-and-swap (PMwCAS) [19] library to realize lock-free index operations.

Tree Structure

BzTree is purely NVM-resident with both inner and leaf nodes in NVM. However it uses different update strategies for them: inner nodes are immutable for inserts and deletes once built (only updates to existing keys and child pointers are allowed), and leaf nodes are mutable. Inner nodes are also sorted, whereas leaf nodes are unsorted (although they are periodically compacted and sorted to optimize for performance). Inserting to an inner node (e.g., as a result of a leaf split) will therefore require allocating a new node which replaces the old node in the tree structure. For leaf nodes, new records and updates are first appended in the free space and are later consolidated with other records to form a sorted leaf node. The rationale for using immutable inner nodes and mutable leaf nodes is that inner nodes should be optimized for (binary)

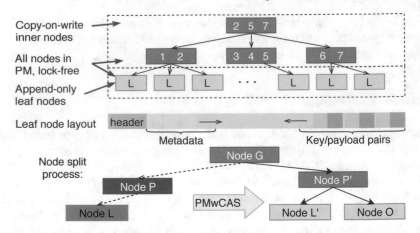

Fig. 4.4: Overview of BzTree. Taken from [13], published under CC BY-NC-ND 4.0, reprinted with permission.

search and are less frequently updated, while leaf nodes should be optimized for write operations.

Lock-Free Index Operations

It is well known that lock-free programming is notoriously hard, although it can bring performance boost under some scenarios. To mitigate this issue, instead of directly employing atomic instructions such as CAS, BzTree uses PMwCAS [19] which is a general-purpose library that aims to simplify lock-free NVM programming. It allows developers to specify a set of 8-byte NVM words and change them atomically following the CAS semantic. That is, all the specified words will be changed if the old value of each specified word matches what was actually stored in NVM. PMwCAS itself is based upon the earlier volatile MwCAS [6] with additional considerations for persistence and crash recovery on NVM. PMwCAS allows BzTree to atomically change multiple NVM pointers during operations such as splits and merges. PMwCAS also transparently supports crash recovery, eliminating the need for BzTree itself to devise complex logic for logging and recovery, further simplifying implementation.

4.3 Optane-Era NVM Range Indexes

The release of Optane PMem in 2019 renewed the interests on devising NVM-based range indexes. While most NVM range indexes proposed before this was based on B+-trees, with Optane more range index types are explored, including radix trees and hybrid structures. The high-level principle remains reducing unnecessary NVM

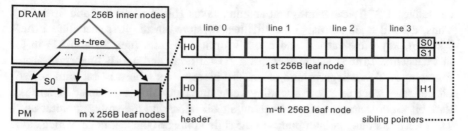

Fig. 4.5: The architecture of LB$^+$-Tree. Taken from [7], published under CC BY-NC-ND 4.0, reprinted with permission.

accesses, but they are also more tailored for the particular device (Optane PMem) which can be a double-edged sword in terms of general applicability; we will come back to this pointer in later chapters. Some indexes also went beyond designing for the "low-hanging fruit" of optimizing short, fixed-length keys on a single NUMA node, to designing for variable length keys and mitigating NUMA effect. In the following, we will take a deep look at five Optane-era NVM range indexes, including LB$^+$-Tree [14], DPTree [22], ROART [16] and PACTree [17].

4.3.1 LB$^+$-Tree

LB$^+$-Tree [14] was proposed primarily to exploit the unique features of Optane PMem, with a particular focus on enhancing insertion performance. For Optane PMem, the write performance is not affected by the number of modified NVM words in an NVM line write. Therefore, LB$^+$-Tree aims to reduce the number of NVM line writes rather than NVM word writes. LB$^+$-Tree sets the tree node size to be 256B or a multiple of 256B, because Optane PMem internally uses 256-byte blocks and delivers better memory bandwidth with 256B reads. As we will see also in later sections, this is a common design that permeated Optane-era NVM indexes. Apart from these two design principles, LB$^+$-Tree proposes three techniques—entry moving, logless node split and distributed headers—to improve insertion performance. Following the FPTree model, LB$^+$-Tree combines hardware transactional memory (HTM) and leaf node locks for concurrency control.

Tree Structure

As a B+-tree variant, LB$^+$-Tree's tree structure largely follows that of FPTree's, by placing inner nodes in DRAM (no persistence) and leaf nodes in NVM (with persistence). This means LB$^+$-Tree also inherits the tradeoff between recovery time and runtime performance from FPTree. Figure 4.5 shows the overall design. All nodes are aligned at 256B boundaries. A 256B node is divided into four 64-byte cachelines. LB$^+$-Tree assumes that an entry takes 16B (i.e., 8B key and 8B value). Thus, a 256B node consists of a 16B header stored in the first cacheline line0, 14× 16B key-value entries, and two 8B sibling pointers (i.e., S0 and S1) in the last cacheline line3. The header has a 1B bit array and a 14B fingerprint array, following FPTree's fingerprinting idea. The bit array contains a 14-bit bitmap. Each bit indicates whether a corresponding key-value entry slot is occupied. There is a lock bit for concurrency control and an alt bit indicating the sibling pointer used. The effective sibling pointer points to the right sibling of the leaf node, which could be NULL for the rightmost leaf node. Each key has a 1B hash value stored in the fingerprint array. Therefore, a 16B SIMD instruction can compare a target key with the fourteen 1B fingerprints to quickly find the slot that is a match, if it exists. As we have mentioned, the overall architecture of LB$^+$-Tree resembles FPTree's, but it further proposes several important designs tailored for Optane PMem, which we describe below.

Entry Moving

An insertion needs to update the header and insert a new entry. Upon insert, LB$^+$-Tree tries to insert the record into line0 if there is an empty slot in it. For line0, only one NVM line write is needed to persist both the header and the new entry, as they are co-located. Otherwise, if line0 is full, the insert will find an empty slot in another line in the leaf node and cause two NVM line writes: one to update the header, the other to write the new entry. LB$^+$-Tree takes this opportunity to move data from line0 to the same cacheline where the new entry is inserted. This approach proactively spares empty slots in line0, which reduces NVM writes in subsequent inserts.

Logless Node Split

Node split is a major performance bottleneck during insertion in traditional B+-trees as it relies on logging to ensure crash consistency, resulting in additional NVM writes. LB$^+$-Tree proposes logless node split to remove the need for logging and extra NVM writes. Upon split, a new leaf node is first allocated and pointed by the unused sibling pointer, which is invisible to concurrent queries. Then, half of entries in the old leaf node are copied to the last two cachelines of the new leaf node to reduce future NVM writes for the new leaf node. Then LB$^+$-Tree uses NVM atomic write to update the leaf header, which flips the alt bit to switch the sibling pointers and clears bits in the bitmap in the old leaf in one go. Therefore, no logging is required during node split.

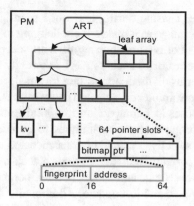

Fig. 4.6: The architecture of ROART. Taken from [7], published under CC BY-NC-ND 4.0, reprinted with permission.

Distributed Headers

To support multi-256B nodes, a naive approach is to still store all metadata in a centralized header at the beginning of the node, i.e. line0 of the first 256 bytes. However, as the node size increases, the header takes up more space, leaving fewer entry slots in the first cacheline, and in the worst case, no entry slot at all. In other words, an insert can hardly update the header and insert the new entry in an NVM line write, regardless of the entry moving optimization. LB⁺-Tree suggests the distributed header technique. That is, it distributes a piece of the header to each 256B block in the node. Like the 256B node, the first block has the lock bit and the alt bit in the header, and two sibling pointers at the end. However, it seems that updating distributed headers now requires multiple NVM writes, and thus requires logging in place. LB⁺-Tree solves this problem by using alternative headers. Starting with the second block of a multi-256B node, the last 16 bytes of each block are used to store the block's alternate header instead of the sibling pointers. LB⁺-Tree reuses the alt bit to indicate whether the front or back header is in use. During a logless node split, LB⁺-Tree writes to the unused headers and performs an NVM atomic write to the first header to switch the sibling pointers in the first block and the headers in the remaining blocks.

4.3.2 ROART

Different from the previously discussed indexes which are all based on B+-trees, ROART [16] is range-query optimized adaptive radix tree (ART) for NVM. Both variable-length keys and range queries are important in real world systems, but neither B+-trees nor ART can manage both features effectively in one structure. B+-trees facilitate efficient range queries because they store multiple keys in a single leaf node, which eliminates pointer chasing during leaf node scans. However, this compact structure is also a disadvantage as it makes it challenging to support variable-length keys. The scan throughput of B+-trees can significantly decrease for variable-length keys. Compared to B+-trees, tries such as ART inherently support variable-length keys well, but range queries on them necessitate traversals across different levels of the index, resulting in more pointer chasing and cache misses. ROART begins with an ART structure and proposes leaf compaction to optimize the performance of range queries. ROART also proposes three techniques to reduce persistence overhead, i.e., entry compression, selective metadata persistence and minimally ordered split. To make the structure correct, ROART employs a lock-free read and lock-based write concurrency control scheme and adopts non-temporal store to fix the potential anomalies, such as dirty read and lost update. Additionally, ROART proposes a new memory allocator (delayed check memory management, DCMM) to ensure memory safety upon failures and speed up the recovery process.

Tree Structure

Figure 4.6 shows the overall architecture of ROART. ROART is fully in NVM. Similar to NV-Tree [20], it selectively persists metadata while the rest can be restored during recovery. For scan optimization, ROART employs consolidates small sub-trees (with fewer than 64 entries) into leaf arrays that hold pointers to records, which minimizes the overhead caused by pointer chasing overhead, makes the index shallower and leads to better CPU cache utilization overall. However, there is a drawback to this method: the cost of splits increases because all the keys in a leaf array are divided into subsets based on the first differing byte, which is followed by a node allocation for each subset. Additional NVM writes and fences are necessary, which increases the workload on the NVM allocator. ROART addresses this issue by minimizing the number of fences through the relaxation of split step order and employing a depth field for inconsistency detection and resolution. It also proposes its own DCMM allocator to cope with the high NVM allocation demand instead of relying on standard PMDK. DCMM utilizes thread-local pools for swift allocations but defers garbage collection until a later stage by traversing the entire index, which may result in higher NVM usage. As ROART is entirely based in NVM, it provides genuine instant recovery support and efficiently handles variable-length keys through its trie-based design, eliminating the need for extra pointer chasing.

Leaf Compaction

To improve range query performance, ROART proposes leaf compaction to reduce pointer chasing. ROART compacts the pointers of unsorted leaf nodes into a leaf array. A leaf array can contain up to m leaf pointers. If a subtree of the radix tree has fewer than or equal to m leaf nodes, the subtree is compacted into a leaf array. Leaf compaction effectively reduces the number of pointer chasing in the different levels of the tree for range queries. To reduce the overhead of probing within a leaf array for the matching leaf node, ROART embeds a 16-bit fingerprint (i.e., hash value of a key) in the leaf array pointer, leaving 48 bits for the pointer per se. Note that when ROART was proposed, x86 CPUs only require 48 bits for addressing, therefore leaving 16 bits for software to (ab)use. However, this has been changing and the latest Intel Sapphire Rapids CPUs already use up to 57 bits for addressing. Therefore, such designs may see limited applicability in the future. With fingerprints, ROART can quickly check if the target key exists in the leaf array. When splitting a full leaf array, ROART needs to divide the associated keys into different subsets, each corresponding to a different leaf array. The subsets are formed based on the first byte where the keys diverge, called the identifying byte. Keys with the same identifying byte are grouped together. For example, to split a leaf array with keys: (1) 12345678, (2) 12345679, (3) 12346678 and (4) 12346679, (1) and (2) will go into the same leaf array, (3) and (4) will go into a different one.

Reducing Persistence Overhead

ROART reduces persistence overhead by using entry compression, selective metadata persistence and minimally ordered split:

1. **Entry Compression and Selective Metadata Persistence.** ROART proposes entry compression that compresses the 1-byte partial keys into the corresponding child pointers of inner nodes, specifically for node types N4, N16 and N48 [11]. Such a pointer with an embedded partial key is referred to as a Zentry. As zentries are 8-byte long, they can be updated and persisted atomically, saving clwb and sfence instructions for persisting the partial keys. The selective metadata persistence technique selectively persists metadata to reduce NVM writes. Metadata that can be rebuilt from zentries (e.g., byte array in N4 or N16 and child index in N48) and should be cleared upon crash recovery (e.g., lock bits) is not persisted.

2. **Minimally Ordered Split.** ROART reduces the number of fences by relaxing the order of internal node split steps. Internal node splitting is costly and involves four steps: (1) allocating a new leaf, (2) allocating a new internal node with two children (the new leaf and the existing internal node), (3) making the pointer in the parent node of the existing node point to the new internal node, and (4) updating the prefix of the existing internal node. Without minimally ordered split, the four steps must be performed in order, and each step requires a fence. ROART observes that step (1) and step (2) are not visible to other threads, therefore only one sfence is required after initializing the two nodes. The order of step (3) and step (4) can be relaxed, because in the case of a crash, the prefix of the existing internal node can be recomputed and repaired [10]. Therefore, minimally ordered split performs step (1), (2) and (4), flushes the modified cachelines, and then invokes sfence. After that, it performs step (3) followed by a cacheline flush and another sfence. Overall, minimally ordered split reduces the number of sfence by half for an internal node split.

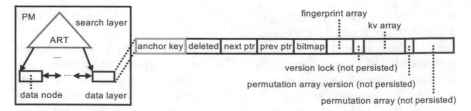

Fig. 4.7: The architecture of PACTree. Taken from [7], published under CC BY-NC-ND 4.0, reprinted with permission.

Delayed Check Memory Management (DCMM)

ROART proposes DCMM to reduce performance overhead from NVM allocation and garbage collection. DCMM uses thread-local allocators to reduce contention in memory allocation. Each thread-local allocator does post-crash epoch-based garbage collection to support lock-free reads and lazy deletions. DCMM also uses a new technique called instant restart to ensure memory safety in case of system failure without long recovery time. More specifically, a global offset is persisted to NVM, which indicates the offset of the last allocated memory page. Upon restart, ROART can immediately allocate new pages after the offset without waiting for other metadata recovery to complete. Full recovery is then performed in the background.

4.3.3 PACTree

PACTree [17] is an NVM-based high performance range index following the Packed Asynchronous Concurrency (PAC) guidelines. Corroborating with prior findings [13], PAC guidelines stress that (1) the limited NVM bandwidth is a key performance-limiting factor for an NVM-based index, and (2) the prolonged blocking time when doing structure modification operations (SMOs) in NVM is a major scalability bottleneck. Therefore, an NVM-based index should perform packed NVM access to save bandwidth and leverage asynchronous concurrency control to reduce blocking time.

Tree Structure

Like ROART, PACTree is also NVM-only, but follows the PAC guidelines to introduce a hybrid tree structure that uses trie-based inner nodes (search layer) and B+-tree-based leaf nodes (data layer). Figure 4.7 shows the overall architecture of PACTree. The trie structure in the search layer uses less bandwidth than B+-tree as it stores partial keys at each level. It is built on concurrent ART, which incorporates read-optimized write exclusion (ROWEX) [12]. Since the search layer is located in

NVM, PACTree can achieve near-instant recovery and excellent capacity scalability. The data layer is a doubly-linked list of B+-tree-like leaf nodes, each of which contains 64 key-value pairs and an anchor key to indicate the smallest key in the node. B+-tree-style leaf nodes decrease NVM allocation overhead as each leaf node holds multiple keys, thereby accelerating scan operations. Sequential reads to a leaf node can take advantage of CPU-level and NVM-level hardware prefetchers, mitigating NVM access latency. To implement non-blocking SMOs, PACTree separates the search layer and the data layer, allowing PACTree to update the search layer asynchronously when an SMO on a leaf node occurs, allowing more concurrent accesses at the cost of using more background threads.

PACTree stores fingerprints and permutation arrays in leaf nodes to facilitate search and scan, but they are not persisted to reduce NVM writes. The permutation array stores indices of the keys of a data node in a sorted manner. This allows for faster scanning. Before a scan, the permutation array is rebuilt on demand by comparing the version lock and the permutation array version. Then, the scan can be performed by reading the keys in the order indexed by the permutation array. The anchor key is the smallest key in the leaf node. The 8-byte bitmap in the leaf node header indicates the validity of a key-value slot.

Asynchronous SMOs

Since the data layer is a doubly-linked list of B+-tree-like data nodes, there are no cascading split and merge operations in the data layer. Instead, the parent node of the newly created data node or deleted data node will be updated in the search layer. During a split, a writer obtains the node lock and logs the split information in a per-thread SMO log. Once the SMO log entry is persisted, the writer allocates a new data node. To avoid NVM leaks, the persistent pointer of the new node is atomically persisted at the placeholder in the SMO log entry. During a merge, PACTree merges the right data node to the left data node where a key is being deleted. PACTree first acquires the locks of the two merging nodes, and then logs the merge information to the per-thread SMO log. A background updater thread replays SMO log entries to update the search layer. It merges and sorts per-thread SMO log entries in timestamp order. Then it replays the entries, inserting the split node's anchor key and deleting the merged node's anchor key in the search layer. PACTree uses epoch-based memory reclamation techniques to ensure that no thread is reading the merged node. This allows worker threads to commit early right after modifying leaf nodes. However, it also creates inconsistencies between the search and data layers. Thus, query threads may need to perform a "last-mile" search after arriving at the data layer to find the correct leaf node using anchor keys. Note that offloading SMOs to the background is not a panacea, especially in resource constrained environments or those with a fixed budget, such as the cloud, using any additional thread (foreground or background) would mean either to pay higher costs (if the number of foreground threads remains the same), or lower query performance (if some foreground threads have to be "drafted" to become background resizing threads) because the total budget (virtual cores) is fixed for a given budget. The application therefore needs to carefully consider budget and compute resource allocation when using indexes that require background threads.

NUMA-Aware NVM Management

PACTree is the only index in this chapter that attempted to mitigate NUMA effect. The basic idea is to use separate NVM pools for the search layer, data layer and logs in each NUMA node. Each NVM pool consists of NUMA-local pools. PACTree always allocates NVM memory from a NUMA-local pool to reduce cross-NUMA traffic. It also advocates the use of snooping-based CPU coherence protocols (instead of the default directory-based protocol on most platforms) to avoid poor performance when NVM accesses cross NUMA boundaries. Despite the NUMA-aware design, as recent work has pointed out, in practice NUMA effect remains to be a major performance bottleneck for NVM indexes and a future direction that requires more attention [7].

4.3.4 DPTree

Having discussed B+-tree and trie variants on NVM, now we look at DPTree [22], a hybrid of B+-tree and trie. DPTree is designed specifically for hybrid DRAM-NVM systems. To reduce NVM writes, it employs flush-optimized persistent logging and crash-consistent in-place merge. The merge algorithm relies on coarse-grained versioning to provide crash-consistency while facilitating concurrent reads.

Tree Structure

As depicted in Figure 4.8, DPTree represents a hybrid index that merges up to two B+-trees (referred to as the *front* and *middle* buffer trees) in DRAM, along with a trie (*base* tree) that stores inner nodes in DRAM and leaf nodes in NVM. When searching for a key, DPTree initially accesses the front buffer tree. If the desired key is not located there, it proceeds to search the middle buffer tree (if it exists). If the key is still not found in the buffer trees, the base tree must be searched. DPTree employs a bloom filter for each buffer tree to reduce unnecessary traversals during key searches. For range queries, DPTree needs to search and combine results from all the trees. DPTree establishes a new front buffer tree and converts the former front buffer tree into a middle buffer tree once the size ratio between the front buffer tree and base tree reaches a predetermined threshold. When the size ratio between the front buffer tree and the base tree meets a predefined threshold, tree merge operations are activated and carried out by background threads. By utilizing the version number and an additional set of metadata, DPTree guarantees that changes remain imperceptible to

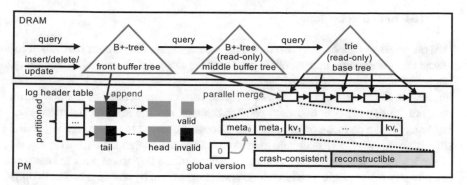

Fig. 4.8: The architecture of DPTree. Taken from [7], published under CC BY-NC-ND 4.0, reprinted with permission.

concurrent queries while a merge operation is underway. Following the completion of the merging process, the middle buffer tree is removed, and the inner nodes of the base tree are reconstructed. Subsequently, the global version bit is toggled to reveal the changes to incoming requests. Next, we take a look at the key techniques proposed by DPTree.

Flush-Optimized Persistent Logging

DPTree assumes that the key-value entries are fixed-length. It maintains a persistent linked list of log records. Usually, a log-append operation necessitates at least two *persist* to ensure crash consistency: one for the log record and another for the link pointer. DPTree, however, relies on the 8B failure-atomic write. Specifically, a validity bit is reserved for every 8B word at the time of log buffer allocation. The system serializes a log record (key-value entry) into several 8B words, each containing 63-bit information and a validity bit (e.g., 0 represents invalid, while 1 signifies valid). These words are subsequently written into the log buffer before being persisted. If a record fits into a 64B cacheline post-serialization, this log-append requires only one *persist*, considering Optane PMem supports cacheline write granularity. Torn writes can be detected when reading the log during recovery by checking the validity bits of log records. As the buffer tree might expand in capacity, the log buffer also needs to accommodate this growth. Once a merge for the buffer tree is completed, the full pages used by the current buffer tree can be recycled for the next buffer tree. Only when the log buffer allocator exhausts free pages does it get filled with pages from the system allocator. In concurrent DPTree, logs are hash partitioned by key into smaller partitions. Each partition is a concurrent persistent linked list of log pages and is equipped with a log buffer allocator.

Coarse-Grained Versioning

DPTree proposes the coarse-grained versioning technique. This is because the before-merge and after-merge images of its base tree naturally set a versioning boundary. Each leaf node has two sets of metadata and a key-value slot pool, as shown in Figure 4.8. Each metadata consists of a bitmap which keeps track of the allocation status of the key-value slots, a next pointer, the max key in the node, the number of key values in the node, an order array that stores the ordered indices to the key-value slots to accelerate range scan, and an array of fingerprints that stores 1-byte hashes of the keys stored at the corresponding positions of the key-value pool to filter out unnecessary NVM reads. The key-value pool is organized by hashing, and collisions are resolved using linear probing. To support deletion in the hash table, each slot is represented by two bits in the bitmap: 00 for empty slot, 01 for occupied slot, and 10 for deleted slot. Hash probing continues until either a matching key or an empty slot is found. A persistent global version gv indicates which set of metadata is active. During the merge, the update of a key-value entry is mostly out-of-place, but within the same leaf. The empty or deleted slots within the leaf are used for the out-of-place updates. The inactive set of metadata keeps track of the out-of-place updates, while the active metadata continues to serve the concurrent queries with the original consistent version. When the merge is complete, DPTree only needs to flip gv to switch the metadata to serve the incoming queries with the updated leaf node, which thus guarantees crash consistency.

Crash-Consistent In-Place Merge

Since the base tree is in NVM, the merge needs to be crash-consistent. One way to implement merge is to merge buffer tree and base tree into a new base tree. However, this method results in high write amplification. Besides, to maintain fast recovery, the merge threshold tends to be a small number to eagerly merge the buffer tree with the base tree, which makes write amplification even worse. The out-of-place merge (i.e., making a new base tree) is optimized for HDD/SSD but not for NVM. Instead, DPTree merges the buffer tree into the base tree in-place to reduce NVM writes. The merge operation uses coarse-grained versioning technique to guarantee crash consistency. During the merge, a pair of iterators is given, which ranges the ordered key-value entries from the buffer tree. The first step is to get the current version cv from gv and compute the next/inactive version nv. Only base tree leaves of version cv undergo merge. Then, the in_merge bit of gv is persistently set to indicate the presence of a merge. During recovery, if in_merge is set, it can tell if a crash happens during merge. Then the merge algorithm goes through the following 7 stages.

1. **Upsert Merge:** The current set of metadata $meta[cv]$ is copied into the next/inactive set of metadata $meta[nv]$. The entries from the buffer tree whose keys are no greater than the max key of the leaf that is currently being handled $Leaf_{cur}$ will be merged into the free slots of $Leaf_{cur}$ that are associated with $meta[nv]$. If there are not enough free slots for the incoming entries, a node

split is required. DPTree first creates as many new leaves as needed to fill in the incoming entries. The new leaves are linked, and the inactive metadata in the previous leaf of $Leaf_{cur}$ will be modified to connect to the first new leaf, and the last one will connect to the next leaf of $Leaf_{cur}$. DPTree can still recover from the current version of each leaf after a system failure, as only the inactive metadata $meta[nv]$ and the slots associated with it are modified during the split. DPTree do not fill the new leaves fully, conforming to a filling rate between 0.5 and 1, as a higher filling rate can result in excessive splits in future merges.

2. **Delete Merge:** For deletion, it only needs to update the bitmap marking the entries as deleted and then reconstruct version nv.

3. **Consolidation:** To maintain adequate node occupancy, leaves from version nv with occupancy below a consolidation threshold merge with adjacent nodes. If sufficient free slots are available, they merge into the next leaf; otherwise, entries are borrowed from the subsequent leaf until both leaves have approximately equal occupancy.

4. **Flush to NVM:** DPTree flushes cachelines that contain newly inserted entries for all leaves of version nv. Since deletion only needs the bitmap to be flushed, cachelines that only contain newly deleted entries are not flushed. Metadata also needs to be flushed. DPTree significantly reduces the number of fences by not enforcing the order of the aforementioned flushes, because only one $mfence$ is required in the upcoming Global Version Flip stage, which guarantees the previous writes are already persisted.

5. **Rebuild Volatile Internal Nodes:** Internal nodes are reconstructed from the leaves of version nv using each leaf's max key and persistent address.

6. **Flip The Global Version:** gv is flipped and persisted to NVM, which officially concludes the merge and frees up the space occupied by the old entries.

7. **Garbage Collection:** Garbage collection must wait until all changes are persisted, so it happens after the global version flip. Garbage leaves may be generated after the previous steps. For example, an old leaf becomes obsolete after a split. To find the garbage leaves, DPTree gets the set of leaves S_{cv} that have a version of cv, and the set of leaves S_{nv} that have a version of nv. So the set of garbage leaves is $S_{cv} - S_{nv}$. To handle crashes during reclamation, DPTree traverses the leaves of version cv backwards, deletes every node in $S_{cv} - S_{nv}$, and then re-executes reclamation.

4.4 Chapter Notes

B+-trees have received the most attention from research communities to devise range indexes on NVM. While we have covered eight range indexes designed for NVM, there are also numerous other proposals since the field is still fast evolving. Some work [21] has targeted eADR to optimize NVM-based B+-trees. Other data structures have also been adapted to work on NVM. For example, UPSkipList [5] adapts the classic lock-free skip list by Herlihy et al [8]. APEX [15] adapts useful techniques from NVM indexes for learned indexes [9] to work well on NVM. NVM indexes are also the building blocks of key-values stores for NVM. NVSkipList [2] is a key-value store that also adapts skip lists for NVM as its main index. The idea of NVSkipList resembles that of many NVM trees, by placing the upper layers of skip lists in DRAM and placing the lowest layer in NVM.

References

[1] Arulraj, J., Levandoski, J.J., Minhas, U.F., Larson, P.: BzTree: A High-Performance Latch-free Range Index for Non-Volatile Memory. PVLDB **11**(5), 553–565 (2018)

[2] Chen, Q., Lee, H., Kim, Y., Yeom, H.Y., Son, Y.: Design and Implementation of Skiplist-Based Key-Value Store on Non-Volatile Memory. Cluster Computing **22**(2), 361–371 (2019)

[3] Chen, S., Gibbons, P.B., Nath, S.: Rethinking Database Algorithms for Phase Change Memory. In: CIDR (2011)

[4] Chen, S., Jin, Q.: Persistent B+-Trees in Non-Volatile Main Memory. PVLDB **8**(7), 786–797 (2015)

[5] Chowdhury, S., Golab, W.: A Scalable Recoverable Skip List for Persistent Memory. In: Proceedings of the 33rd ACM Symposium on Parallelism in Algorithms and Architectures, SPAA '21, p. 426–428. Association for Computing Machinery, New York, NY, USA (2021)

[6] Harris, T.L., Fraser, K., Pratt, I.A.: A Practical Multi-Word Compare-and-Swap Operation. In: Proceedings of the 16th International Conference on Distributed Computing, DISC '02, p. 265–279. Springer-Verlag, Berlin, Heidelberg (2002)

[7] He, Y., Lu, D., Huang, K., Wang, T.: Evaluating Persistent Memory Range Indexes: Part Two. Proc. VLDB Endow. **15**(11), 2477–2490 (2022)

[8] Herlihy, M., Shavit, N.: The Art of Multiprocessor Programming, Revised Reprint, 1st edn. Morgan Kaufmann Publishers Inc., San Francisco, CA, USA (2012)

[9] Kraska, T., Beutel, A., Chi, E.H., Dean, J., Polyzotis, N.: The Case for Learned Index Structures. In: SIGMOD, p. 489–504 (2018)

[10] Lee, S.K., Lim, K.H., Song, H., Nam, B., Noh, S.H.: WORT: Write Optimal Radix Tree for Persistent Memory Storage Systems. In: 15th USENIX Conference on File and Storage Technologies (FAST 17), pp. 257–270. USENIX Association, Santa Clara, CA (2017)

[11] Leis, V., Kemper, A., Neumann, T.: The Adaptive Radix Tree: ARTful Indexing for Main-Memory Databases. In: Proceedings of the 2013 IEEE International Conference on Data Engineering, ICDE '13, p. 38–49 (2013)

[12] Leis, V., Scheibner, F., Kemper, A., Neumann, T.: The ART of Practical Synchronization. In: Proceedings of the 12th International Workshop on Data Management on New Hardware, DaMoN '16 (2016)

[13] Lersch, L., Hao, X., Oukid, I., Wang, T., Willhalm, T.: Evaluating Persistent Memory Range Indexes. PVLDB **13**(4), 574–587 (2019)

[14] Liu, J., Chen, S., Wang, L.: LB+Trees: Optimizing Persistent Index Performance on 3DXPoint Memory. PVLDB **13**(7), 1078–1090 (2020)

[15] Lu, B., Ding, J., Lo, E., Minhas, U.F., Wang, T.: APEX: A High-Performance Learned Index on Persistent Memory. PVLDB **15**(3), 597–610 (2021)

[16] Ma, S., Chen, K., Chen, S., Liu, M., Zhu, J., Kang, H., Wu, Y.: ROART: Range-query Optimized Persistent ART. In: 19th USENIX Conference on File and Storage Technologies (FAST 21), pp. 1–16. USENIX Association (2021)

[17] Ma, S., Chen, K., Chen, S., Liu, M., Zhu, J., Kang, H., Wu, Y.: ROART: Range-query Optimized Persistent ART. In: 19th USENIX Conference on File and Storage Technologies (FAST 21), pp. 1–16. USENIX Association (2021)

[18] Oukid, I., Lasperas, J., Nica, A., Willhalm, T., Lehner, W.: FPTree: A Hybrid SCM-DRAM Persistent and Concurrent B-Tree for Storage Class Memory. In: Proceedings of the 2016 International Conference on Management of Data, SIGMOD '16, p. 371–386. Association for Computing Machinery, New York, NY, USA (2016)

[19] Wang, T., Levandoski, J., Larson, P.A.: Easy lock-free indexing in non-volatile memory. In: 2018 IEEE 34th International Conference on Data Engineering (ICDE), pp. 461–472 (2018)

[20] Yang, J., Wei, Q., Chen, C., Wang, C., Yong, K.L., He, B.: NV-Tree: Reducing Consistency Cost for NVM-based Single Level Systems. In: 13th USENIX Conference on File and Storage Technologies (FAST 15), pp. 167–181. USENIX Association, Santa Clara, CA (2015)

[21] Zhang, B., Zheng, S., Qi, Z., Huang, L.: Nbtree: a lock-free pm-friendly persistent b+-tree for eadr-enabled pm systems. PVLDB **15**(6), 1187–1200 (2022)

[22] Zhou, X., Shou, L., Chen, K., Hu, W., Chen, G.: DPTree: Differential Indexing for Persistent Memory. PVLDB **13**(4), 421–434 (2019)

Chapter 5
Hash Tables on Non-Volatile Memory

Abstract This chapter surveys hashing techniques for NVM. Hash tables on NVM also have to depart from traditional in-memory or on-disk hashing architectures to consider NVM's properties, such as limited endurance and lower performance compared to DRAM.

5.1 Introduction

While tree-based solutions support all the index operations (especially range queries), they may not offer superior point query performance. This chapter discusses how hash tables—which arguably are among the best for point queries—can be designed to work well on NVM. Similar to their DRAM and SSD counterparts, NVM-based hash tables can be categorized as static or dynamic, depending on whether resizing would require full-table rehashing. Both types of NVM hash tables pay much attention to reducing unnecessary NVM accesses via better designs of the hash table structure and algorithms that handle issues such as concurrency control and collisions. In addition, dynamic hash tables are often adaptations of their SSD counterparts, such as the extendible hashing and linear hashing algorithms described in Chapter 3. As we will see later in this chapter, techniques from NVM range indexes such as fingerprinting are also useful for hash tables on NVM.

While the quality of hash functions remains important, the NVM-based hash table designs we describe in this chapter focus on the actual hash table architecture design that is largely orthogonal to hash functions which are assumed to lead to uniform random key distributions.

In the rest of this chapter, we take a deep look into both types of NVM-based hash tables through the lens of hash table structure, consistency guarantees, concurrency control, load factor, resizing, instant recovery and variable-length key support. Again, we begin with pre-Optane solutions, followed by Optane-era solutions.

© The Author(s), under exclusive license to Springer Nature Switzerland AG 2024
K. Huang, T. Wang, *Indexing on Non-Volatile Memory*, SpringerBriefs in Computer Science,
https://doi.org/10.1007/978-3-031-47627-3_5

5.2 Level Hashing

Level hashing [12] starts with a traditional static hashing scheme and proposes several designs to optimize it for NVM. It is fully NVM-resident and does not require DRAM to store hash table components. Like many other pre-Optane indexes, its main goal was to reduce unnecessary writes and maintain consistency and recoverability. This is realized through a new two-level hash table structure, new resizing algorithms and cheaper approaches to consistency guarantees.

Hash Table Structure

A significant issue of traditional static hashing is that it handles collisions poorly and can lead to low space utilization (load factor) under skewed workloads. If collisions are not handled well, then expansion would be necessary which subsequently causes full-table rehashing. Level hashing proposes a two-level structure, along with several tweaks to improve load factor and delay such full-table rehashing. Figure 5.1 shows the two-level structure which consists of a top level and a bottom level. Each level consists of a fixed number of buckets, each of which consists of multiple slots for storing records (key-value pairs). Within the bucket, a lookup operation performs a linear search to find the target key.

The top level is what we would take as "the hash table" in a traditional design as described in Chapter 3.3 and is directly addressable via the hash function. The bottom level consists of another set of buckets, which are not directly used after hashing a key, but as an overflow area for keys that cannot be inserted to the top level. The number of buckets in the bottom level is set to be half of the number of buckets in the top level. Moreover, each pair of buckets (e.g., buckets N and $N+1$) in the top level is matched with a distinct bucket in the bottom level (e.g., bucket B).

Level hashing is based on open addressing and uses two hash functions for each key that respectively give two target buckets: $TL_1 = hash_1(key) \% N$ and $TL_2 = hash_2(key) \% N$. Upon insert, the key is hashed into two potential buckets in the top level, and is inserted to the bucket that is less full. If there is no space in the top level, level hashing finds an available slot in the corresponding bottom-level bucket, using the same hash functions but targeting the bottom level: $BL_1 = hash_1(key) \% (N/2)$ and $BL_2 = hash_2(key) \% (N/2)$. In the worst case, a search operation will need to examine four buckets: two top-level buckets and their corresponding bottom-level buckets. The two levels are stored in separate arrays, allowing accessing the bottom-level bucket from the top level via simple array offsets instead of using pointers dereferencing which can cause many cache misses.

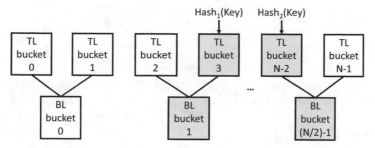

Fig. 5.1: Overview of level hashing. The hash table consists of two layers: the top level (TL) and the bottom level (BL). The former is used for addressing and the latter is used as an overflow area for keys that cannot be inserted to the top level.

Reducing Data Movement during Insert

Level hashing's use of two hash locations for a key bears similarity to cuckoo hashing: Upon collision, the latter evicts and relocates existing records to alternative buckets. This process continues until a vacant slot/bucket is found, which can result in excessive NVM writes. Level hashing mitigates this issue by restricting the number of record movement to be one. When both target buckets in the top and bottom levels are full, level hashing checks if an existing record can be relocated to its alternative top-level bucket in one movement. If so, the insert is completed; otherwise, we resort to the bottom-level. A similar check is performed at the bottom level. If the insert cannot be completed with a single movement of a bottom-level record, the hash table needs to be resized, which we discuss next.

In-Place Resizing

A major dealbreaker for static hashing is that full-table rehashing is necessary when the hash table needs to be resized (to extend or shrink). In an NVM-resident hash table, full-table rehashing would generate many write activities to NVM, leading to low performance and long service downtime. Level hashing proposes an in-place resizing strategy to mitigate this issue. Figure 5.2 shows an example. The hash table initially has N buckets in the top level and $N/2$ buckets in the bottom level. The goal is to expand and rehash the keys into $2N$ buckets in the top level. Subsequently, the bottom level would contain N buckets in the new, expanded hash table. Level hashing first allocates $2N$ buckets for the top level, leading to a temporary three-level structure: the new top level with $2N$ buckets, the previous top level which now is the bottom level (with N buckets) and the previous bottom level which is now regarded as an "interim level." The records in the interim level are then rehashed into the new top level. This way, level hashing reuses the NVM space that was allocated for the previous top level as the new bottom level, significantly reducing NVM writes.

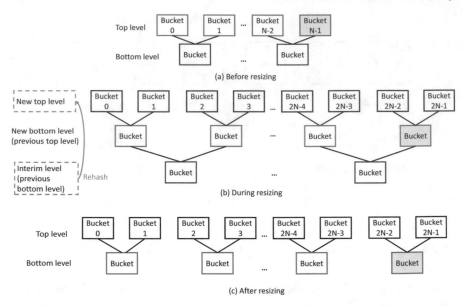

Fig. 5.2: An example of in-place resizing in level hashing. (a) Before resizing, there are four buckets in the top level and two buckets in the lower level. (b) During resizing, a new top layer with $2N$ buckets is created. The previous top level (with N buckets) then becomes the new bottom level, reusing the NVM memory that already exists. (c) The previous bottom level becomes an "interim" level which will be deallocated after the records are rehashed to the new top and bottom levels.

Consistency

Each bucket in level hashing has a header area that stores a "token" per slot to indicate whether the slot represented by the token is empty or already taken to store a record. As shown in Figure 5.3, a token is represented by a 1-bit flag, where 0 denotes an empty slot and 1 denotes a non-empty slot. The size of the header area is 1 byte when the number of slots is 8 or less, so modifying the tokens only requires one atomic NVM write. However, in practice the size of a record (key and value) is usually greater than 8 bytes. Thus, insert, update, and delete operations often have to rely on logging or copy-on-write (CoW) or write-ahead logging mechanisms for consistency. Yet maintaining a log can be heavyweight for (non-volatile) memory-resident data structures. To reduce such overheads for maintaining data consistency, level hashing makes delete, insert and resizing operations completely log-free and makes updates opportunistically log-free.

Log-Free Insert and Delete. Deleting a record is as simple as changing the corresponding token from 1 to 0 in one atomic write, rendering the slot empty. When inserting a new record, there are two possible scenarios:

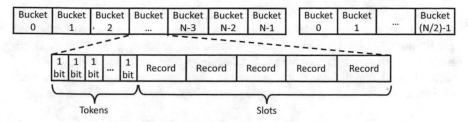

Fig. 5.3: Bucket structure of level hashing.

1. **No record movement.** This occurs when an empty slot is available. As a result, we (1) write the record in the slot and (2) change the token to 1. It is important to maintain this order as otherwise a subsequent query may read inconsistent data. This is accomplished by inserting a memory fence instruction. There is no need for logging or CoW, as the record becomes visible only when the corresponding token is atomically set to 1, regardless of the size of the record.

2. **Moving one record.** This occurs when inserting an record requires moving an existing record. In this case, two steps are taken to insert the record. The first step involves moving an existing record to its alternative bucket, changing the token of the alternative bucket from 0 to 1, and finally changing the token of the current slot from 1 to 0. If a system failure occurs during the copying operation, the hash table will contain two duplicate records. However, this duplication does not affect data consistency. When updating this record, one of the duplicates is first deleted, and then the other one is updated, which we will explain in opportunistic log-free update later. After moving the existing record, the second step simply follows the approach described in the other scenario where no record movement is needed.

Log-Free Resizing. During resizing, an record in the interim bucket is rehashed to a new slot at the top two levels, which is a combination of the aforementioned approaches: log-free insert and log-free deletion. Data consistency is ensured through the following steps:

1. Copy the record from the old slot to the new slot.
2. Change the token of the new slot from 0 to 1.
3. Change the token of the old slot from 1 to 0.

In the case of a system failure, only the first record (I_{first}) to be rehashed at the interim level may be inconsistent. To check for the presence of two duplicates of I_{first} in the hash table, the key of I_{first} is queried at the top-two levels. If two duplicates are found, I_{first} can be directly deleted. Otherwise, the rehashing process continues. This guarantees the data consistency of the recovered hash table.

Opportunistic Log-Free Update. Updates follow a two-step process in level hashing. (1) Check if there is an empty slot in the bucket where the target value v is stored. If an empty slot is found, the new value v' is directly written into the empty slot. Subsequently, the tokens of both v and v' are modified simultaneously. Since the tokens are stored together in an 8-byte word, an atomic write is enough to modify both without consistency issues. Again, the ordering of writing the new record and modifying the tokens is ensured using a fence instruction. (2) If no empty slot is available in the bucket containing v, level hashing then has to use logging where v is first logged, and then the slot is updated in place with the new value. In the event of a system failure during the overwrite process, v can be recovered from the log.

Concurrency Control

Level hashing implements slot-level, fine-grained locking. When a thread accesses (reads or writes) a slot, it first acquires the corresponding lock. As level hashing ensures that each insert moves at most one existing record, an insert operation locks at most two slots: the current slot and the target slot where the record will be moved into. However, the likelihood of an insert requiring record movement is expected to be low. While fine-grained locking is easy to implement and serves its intended purpose, it can be heavyweight and hinder performance. Follow up work [1] alleviates this issue with lock-free approaches which are more complex but provide overall progress guarantees.

5.3 Cacheline-Conscious Extendible Hashing

Different from static hashing based approaches, cacheline-conscious extendible hashing (CCEH) bases on extendible hashing, a classic hashing design for secondary storage devices described in Chapter 3.3.2, to realize graceful resizing while reducing unnecessary NVM accesses. CCEH also presents a failure-atomic rehashing algorithm, along with a recovery algorithm that avoids the need for explicit logging.

Hash Table Structure

Compared to its disk/SSD counterparts, CCEH is specifically designed for low-latency byte-addressable NVM with several improvements aimed at reducing unnecessary NVM writes. An important departure from traditional disk-based extendible hashing is that CCEH uses cacheline-sized buckets to reduce the number of NVM accesses required. For most x86 processors, this leads to 64-byte buckets, which is much smaller than traditional extendible hash tables which usually use storage page sizes as bucket sizes (e.g., 4KB), leading to more buckets needed for a hash table of the same size. Intuitively, using cacheline-sized buckets can reduce unnecessary data transfers between the CPU and NVM as the unit of such transfers is a cacheline

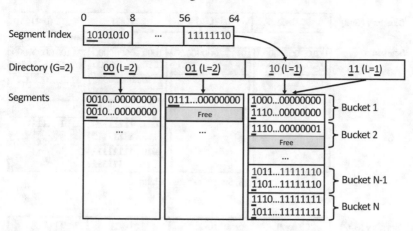

Fig. 5.4: CCEH structure. Compared to traditional extendible hashing, CCEH's directory entries point to segments, instead of individual buckets. Each segment groups multiple buckets. This reduces the size of the directory but may cause premature split which now happens at the segment level.

(64 bytes typically). However, note that since the directory entries directly index buckets, the directory can become prohibitively large. To control the directory size, one may increase bucket size, but this would tradeoff lookup performance since the whole bucket needs to be loaded from NVM to the CPU cache to perform a bucket search. Yet the actually useful data may only be a subset of a cacheline, wasting precious CPU cache space and lowering locality.

To strike a balance between directory size and lookup performance, CCEH introduces the concept of segments: A segment consists of a group of adjacent buckets and directory entries now only point to segments, instead of individual buckets, as shown in Figure 5.4. To access a bucket in this three-level (directory $\rightarrow$ segment $\rightarrow$ bucket) structure, a segment index (represented by G bits, denoting global depth) and a bucket index (determined by B bits, indicating the number of cachelines in a segment) are used to locate the target bucket.

As Figure 5.4 shows, this can significantly reduce directory size. Suppose each bucket can hold two records (indicated by solid lines within the segments), the directory size can be reduced by a factor of $1/2^B$ (1/256 in the example) by using B bits as the bucket index instead of directly addressing each bucket. Given a hash value $10101010...11111110_{(2)}$, we use the first two leading bits (i.e., $10_{(2)}$) as the segment index (global depth = 2) and the least significant byte (i.e., $11111110_{(2)}$) as the bucket index. By accessing the segment using the segment index (Segment 3), we can locate the specific bucket containing the search key using the bucket index ($11111110_{(2)}$). As a result, in total only two cacheline accesses are required to locate a record.

The downside of using segment is that split will happen at the segment level. Although the target bucket does not have enough space to accommodate new keys,

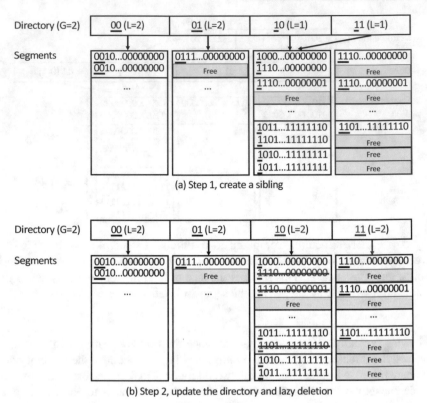

(a) Step 1, create a sibling

(b) Step 2, update the directory and lazy deletion

Fig. 5.5: Failure-atomic segment split in CCEH.

other buckets may still have plenty of space. Yet the segment still has to be split, lowering space utilization (load factor). We describe other proposals such as Dash [6] that can solve this problem later.

Consistency

The main source for potential inconsistency for extendible hashing is directory and segment structure manipulations during structural modification operations (such as segment split and merge) since the unit for atomic NVM accesses is 8-byte. CCEH implements failure-atomic schemes for segment split/merge and directory update.

During a segment split, CCEH creates a new segment and copies records from the split segment based on their hash keys. We explain this process using an example shown in Figure 5.5. Initially, the hash table has three buckets and a global depth of 2. The third segment (Segment 3) has two incoming pointers from the directory (i.e., its local depth is 1), so it is sufficient to use one bit to locate the segment. Suppose our

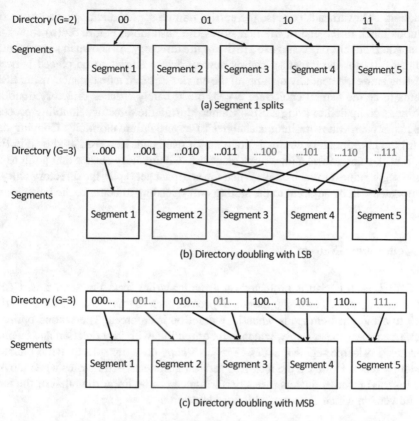

Fig. 5.6: Comparison between using MSB vs. LSB in CCEH to double the directory.

goal is to insert key whose hash value is $1010...11111110_{(2)}$. This leads to the 255th bucket in the third segment (Segment 3) because the MSB is 1. The corresponding bucket, however, is full, mandating a split to make room for the key.

CCEH starts the split process by allocating a new segment (Segment 4 in the figure). It then moves records with a key prefix starting with $11_{(2)}$ from Segment 3 to Segment 4. Following the extendible hashing algorithm introduced earlier, after adding Segment 4, as shown in Figure 5.5(b), the local depth is bumped to 2, same as the global depth. Also, the two directory entries are modified to point to Segments 3 and 4, respectively. This mandates two bits in the hash value to differentiate the two segments. Records in Segment 3 are then scanned, rehashed and redistributed among Segments 3 and 4. Note that the above operations cannot be performed atomically, so a crash when a split is in progress may leave the directory in an inconsistent state. CCEH detects and resolves such inconsistencies in its recovery process.

In Figure 5.6(a), if the segment pointed to by the first directory entry, the directory must be doubled to accommodate the additional segment. For disk-based extendible hashing, using the least significant bits (LSB) allows reusing the directory file and reducing I/O overheads because the entries can be copied and appended as a contiguous block to the end of file that stores the hash table. Figure 5.6(b) shows the idea. Alternatively, one could use MSBs for the directory. As shown in Figure 5.6(c), using MSBs for the directory causes new directory entries to be placed between existing entries, potentially making all the entries dirty. At a first glance, using LSBs seems to be the natural choice for NVM, but it barely reduces directory doubling overhead compared to using MSBs. Rather, during the directory doubling process, the major overhead is flushing cachelines to ensure failure atomicity. Copying data to fill the new directory entries is not a major overhead. However, as shown in Figure 5.6(c), using MSBs allows us to place the two directory entries that point to the same segment next to each other. When the segment gets split, the directory entry to be updated will be adjacent to the sibling entry, leading to better cache behaviour.

Concurrency Control

In CCEH, each bucket is protected by a reader-writer lock. For segments, CCEH offers two options. The first option is to protect each segment using a reader-writer lock to avoid phantom reads when lazy deletion is enforced. The second option is lock-free access to segments, which is incompatible with lazy deletion and in-place updates. Lock-free segment accesses require copy-on-write split to avoid phantom and dirty reads. However, the lock-free version introduces extra writes when moving the inserted records, thus its insert performance can be lower than that of the lock-based version which can work with lazy deletion.

5.4 Dash

Most NVM-based hash tables focused on reducing the amount of NVM writes, based on the assumption that NVM writes in general are slower than NVM reads. While this is indeed the case at the device level because of the characteristics of the hardware itself, it may or may not be always the case end-to-end: as prior work has shown [9], the end-to-end latency of NVM read (in particular Optane PMem) can actually be longer than that of a write. The reason is that while writes typically can enjoy the benefits of CPU caching, read operations, especially random reads, will not benefit much from CPU caches. For hash tables, this becomes critically important because most of the read operations for a hash table are random in nature. It then becomes important to not only optimize for write operations, but also to reduce unnecessary read operations for NVM hash tables, which is a major goal of Dash [6]. Dash also proposes designs for other important features, including variable-length key support, instant recovery and high space utilization.

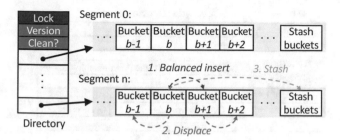

Fig. 5.7: Overall architecture of Dash for extendible hashing. Taken from [6], published under CC BY-NC-ND 4.0, reprinted with permission.

Hash Table Structure

Dash [6] combines several techniques to reduce both reads and writes on NVM. These techniques can be applied on traditional dynamic hashing techniques, including extendible hashing and linear hashing. We take extendible hashing as an example in our discussion as the adaptation for linear hashing is very similar.

The extendible hashing variant of Dash follows largely CCEH's overall architecture, by employing a directory and the segmentation design. As mentioned earlier, a major issue of CCEH's segmentation design is that it is vulnerable to premature splits which can lead to very low space utilization: a segment will split as long as any bucket in the segment is full, yet other buckets may still have a lot of free slots. Dash proposes several important additions to improve both performance and space utilization. Figure 5.7 shows the overall architecture. Dash also places the directory in NVM, making it a fully-NVM solution that does not have to use DRAM. Like CCEH, each directory entry in Dash also points to a segment which consists of multiple buckets. Different from CCEH, however, in Dash each bucket (as shown in Figure 5.8) carries fingerprints to reduce unnecessary reads. The fingerprints here are adopted from FPTree [7]. Dash proposes three improvements to the insert and search algorithms to improve space utilization and delay bucket/segment split. Next, we describe how these techniques work to achieve the goals of reducing unnecessary NVM accesses (reads and writes) and improve space utilization.

Fingerprinting

Fingerprinting was originally adopted by NVM-based B+-trees to allow faster search, as we introduced in Chapter 4. Dash further adapted it to work with hash tables based on the observation that end-to-end read latency on NVM is often higher than that of NVM writes. As shown in Figure 5.8, each bucket in Dash consists of a metadata area, followed by an array of 14 records (key-value pairs). Inside the metadata area, there is a dedicated region of 18 fingerprints, 14 of which correspond to the 14 records stored in this bucket, and the remaining four for records stored in stash

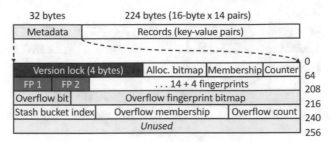

Fig. 5.8: Bucket layout in Dash for extendible hashing. Taken from [6], published under CC BY-NC-ND 4.0, reprinted with permission.

buckets but were originally hashed to this bucket; we discuss the idea of stashing later. The fingerprints here are also one-byte hashes of the keys, exactly the same as those in FPTree. To search for a record with a give key, Dash first hashes the key to obtain at the corresponding bucket (same process as CCEH). It then first reads the fingerprints to check for matches, and linearly searches the record array only if there is a match. This way, Dash reduces unnecessary NVM reads not only for pure lookup operations, but also insert/update operations which also rely on fingerprints to conduct existence check.

Load Balancing

To improve space utilization, Dash proposes three techniques that when combined, can delay segment split. Upon collision during an insert, Dash will attempt the three techniques in order, before a segment split has to be triggered.

The first technique is balanced insert which is a restricted version of linear probing: if the target bucket b is full, Dash also probes bucket $b + 1$ and inserts the record to the bucket that is less full. Compared to original linear probing, Dash limits the probing length to one in order to reduce NVM accesses and save NVM bandwidth.

If balanced insert was unable to find the target key a slot, Dash performs displacement to try to make room for the target record. Suppose the key is originally hashed into bucket b, and bucket $b + 1$ is also full, Dash will try to move a record in bucket $b + 1$ to bucket $b + 2$. If this is still unsuccessful, Dash will retry the process for bucket b but move the record in bucket b to bucket $b - 1$.

If neither balanced insert nor displacement was able to find a slot for the target key, Dash will "stash" the record into one of the stash buckets. Stash buckets use the same layout as "normal" buckets. As Figure 5.7 shows, there is a number of stash buckets following the normal buckets in each segment. Similar to the bottom level of level hashing (Chapter 5.2), the stash buckets here also do not directly participate addressing, but only provide overflow space for records that cannot be inserted into "normal" buckets. Unlike level hashing which fixes the ratio between top and bottom level buckets, the number of stash buckets in Dash can be tuned depending on the workload. The main benefit of stashing is that it can improve load factor. However, stashing can also trade off performance: Using more stash buckets leads to more CPU cycles and NVM bandwidth spent on searching through the stash buckets. Dash employs additional metadata such as overflow fingerprints as shown in Figure 5.8 to accelerate the search of stash buckets. Overall, the combination of these techniques was able to improve throughput by up to ~3× over prior state of the art (CCEH) while maintaining high load factor [6].

Concurrency and Recovery

Unlike prior work which either opted for lock-based or lock-free approaches for concurrency, Dash takes a middle ground to adopt optimistic locking for concurrency control, striking a balance between easy implementation and performance. As shown in Figure 5.8, each bucket has a versioned lock that is only taken by writers (i.e., during update or insert operations) which will atomically increment the version number upon releasing the lock. Readers will only need to record the version number and verify the version number did not change (and the lock is still unlocked) after reading the record.

Since Dash is purely NVM-resident, it can easily support instant recovery. The basic idea is to associate (1) the hash table with a global version number and a `clean` marker (shown in Figure 5.7), and (2) each segment with a local version number. The version numbers and clean marker then allow Dash to tell whether a recovery pass is needed upon restart and during forward processing. The clean marker is a boolean denoting whether the system was previously shut down cleanly. Upon system start, the clean marker is set to false if it is originally true. The system then starts to serve incoming requests. Therefore, if the system was not shutdown cleanly, upon restart the marker will carry `false`, signalling the potential need for recovery work which is done lazily on demand when segments are accessed. If the clean marker is false, Dash bumps the global version by one and then starts forward processing. This way, Dash bounds the amount of recovery work that has to be done before starting to serve requests to a constant: reading the `clean` marker and possibly also incrementing the global version number.

After the bounded number of steps during the recovery phase, Dash amortizes "real" recovery work to forward processing and conducts recovery work on demand as segments are accessed. This is where the segment-level version numbers are used: if they do not match the global version number, that means a recovery pass is needed before the records in the segment can be accessed. After recovery, the segment-local version number will be set to be the same as the global version, allowing subsequent accesses to skip recovery.

5.5 Chapter Notes

There have been even earlier work than the pre-Optane indexes described here, such as PFHT [2] and path hashing [11], but they mostly only focused on reducing NVM writes, rather than other important issues such as maintaining the consistency of the hash table structure and concurrency. Techniques in NVM range indexes such as fingerprinting have been adopted by hash tables. Conversely, techniques from NVM hash tables are also being adopted by range indexes. For example, among Optane-era solutions, APEX [5] (a learned index for NVM) adopted the instant recovery and optimistic concurrency approaches in Dash. Like the case for NVM range indexes, new NVM-based hash tables are also being devised. Plush [10] is another hash table designed for Optane PMem that leverage a bounded amount of DRAM and optimizes for writes by leveraging principles originated from log-structured merge trees. More recent NVM hash tables such as PeaHash [4] added better support for non-unique keys and skewed accesses. IcebergHT [8] is another recent NVM hash table that further optimizes for space efficiency and slow NVM accesses. Beyond individual hash table proposals for NVM, Hu et al. [3] also performed a performance evaluation of NVM-based hash tables, several of which are included in this chapter.

References

[1] Chen, Z., Hua, Y., Ding, B., Zuo, P.: Lock-free Concurrent Level Hashing for Persistent Memory. In: 2020 USENIX Annual Technical Conference (USENIX ATC 20), pp. 799–812. USENIX Association (2020)

[2] Debnath, B., Haghdoost, A., Kadav, A., Khatib, M.G., Ungureanu, C.: Revisiting Hash Table Design for Phase Change Memory. In: Proceedings of the 3rd Workshop on Interactions of NVM/FLASH with Operating Systems and Workloads, INFLOW 2015, Monterey, California, USA, October 4, 2015, pp. 1:1–1:9 (2015)

[3] Hu, D., Chen, Z., Wu, J., Sun, J., Chen, H.: Persistent Memory Hash Indexes: An Experimental Evaluation. Proc. VLDB Endow. **14**(5), 785–798 (2021)

[4] Liu, Z., Chen, S.: Pea Hash: A Performant Extendible Adaptive Hashing Index. Proc. ACM Manag. Data **1**(1) (2023)

[5] Lu, B., Ding, J., Lo, E., Minhas, U.F., Wang, T.: APEX: A High-Performance Learned Index on Persistent Memory. PVLDB **15**(3), 597–610 (2021)

[6] Lu, B., Hao, X., Wang, T., Lo, E.: Dash: Scalable Hashing on Persistent Memory. PVLDB **13**(8), 1147–1161 (2020)

[7] Oukid, I., Lasperas, J., Nica, A., Willhalm, T., Lehner, W.: FPTree: A Hybrid SCM-DRAM Persistent and Concurrent B-Tree for Storage Class Memory. In: Proceedings of the 2016 International Conference on Management of Data, SIGMOD '16, p. 371–386. Association for Computing Machinery, New York, NY, USA (2016)

[8] Pandey, P., Bender, M.A., Conway, A., Farach-Colton, M., Kuszmaul, W., Tagliavini, G., Johnson, R.: IcebergHT: High Performance Hash Tables Through Stability and Low Associativity. Proc. ACM Manag. Data 1(1) (2023)

[9] van Renen, A., Vogel, L., Leis, V., Neumann, T., Kemper, A.: Persistent memory I/O primitives. In: Proceedings of the 15th International Workshop on Data Management on New Hardware, DaMoN 2019., pp. 12:1–12:7 (2019)

[10] Vogel, L., van Renen, A., Imamura, S., Giceva, J., Neumann, T., Kemper, A.: Plush: A Write-Optimized Persistent Log-Structured Hash-Table. Proc. VLDB Endow. 15(11), 2895–2907 (2022)

[11] Zuo, P., Hua, Y.: A Write-Friendly and Cache-Optimized Hashing Scheme for Non-Volatile Memory Systems. IEEE Transactions on Parallel and Distributed Systems 29(5), 985–998 (2018)

[12] Zuo, P., Hua, Y., Wu, J.: Write-Optimized and High-Performance Hashing Index Scheme for Persistent Memory. In: 13th USENIX Symposium on Operating Systems Design and Implementation (OSDI 18), pp. 461–476. USENIX Association, Carlsbad, CA (2018)

Chapter 6
Summary

Abstract This chapter summarizes the previously discussed techniques following several dimensions and distills useful design principles that can be useful for building indexes on NVM and DRAM/SSDs in general.

6.1 Overview

Having looked at the detailed design of various indexes on NVM, now we summarize and distill the common and useful designs. Perhaps unsurprisingly—despite these indexes present vastly different detailed design decisions—their key goal boils to *reducing unnecessary NVM accesses* which has permeated almost our entire discussion in this book. Nevertheless, the actual realization of this principle led to several design points that are useful for NVM indexing. As we discuss later in the next chapter, they can also be useful for building in-memory/far-memory and persistent indexes on SSDs in general.

We categorize the techniques and indexes by their overall architectures, node/bucket layout, concurrency control protocols, NVM management approaches and other functionality. Along the way, we highlight the common design principles, especially the ones that stood the "test of time," i.e., those that were already proposed by pre-Optane indexes (such as NV-Tree, BzTree, FPTree and wB$^+$-Tree) and are further validated to be effective on real Optane PMem later. Some of the discussion in this chapter is based on two previous evaluation studies [3, 5] but focuses more on qualitative comparisons; interested readers are referred to the original papers [3, 5] for performance evaluation studies. For brevity, we limit our discussions to range indexes on NVM as we find hash table design principles largely converge on those of range indexes.

K. Huang, T. Wang, *Indexing on Non-Volatile Memory*, SpringerBriefs in Computer Science,
https://doi.org/10.1007/978-3-031-47627-3_6

Table 6.1: Range NVM index designs. Most indexes are based on B+-trees, leverage DRAM and relax traditional B+-tree node layout to reduce potential NVM accesses. Taken from [3], published under CC BY-NC-ND 4.0, reprinted with permission.

	Baseline	Media	Node Structure
wB+-Tree	B+-tree	NVM-only	Unsorted; indirection
BzTree	B+-tree	NVM-only	Partially unsorted leaf
FPTree	B+-tree	DRAM (inner nodes) + NVM (leaf nodes)	Unsorted leaf; fingerprinting
NV-Tree	B+-tree	NVM-only or DRAM + NVM	Unsorted leaf; inconsistent inner nodes
LB+-Tree	B+-tree	DRAM (inner nodes) + NVM (leaf nodes)	Unsorted leaf; fingerprinting; extra metadata
DPTree	Hybrid	DRAM (B+-tree, trie inner nodes) + NVM (trie leaf nodes)	Unsorted leaf; fingerprinting; extra metadata; indirection
ROART	Trie	NVM-only	Unsorted leaf; fingerprinting
PACTree	Trie	NVM-only or DRAM + NVM	Unsorted leaf; fingerprinting; indirection

6.2 Index Structure and Layout

Most range indexes on NVM take in-memory B+-tree as their baseline and propose further optimizations for their data layout and other aspects to approach in-memory B+-tree performance on DRAM. We summarize these design choices in Table 6.1. A few proposals have used trie (radix tree) structures (for example, to get better string key support) and hybrid of trees, tries and linked lists. They typically face a different set of tradeoffs compared to B+-tree based NVM indexes as we have covered in previous chapters.

As a direct answer to the question of how to reduce unnecessary NVM accesses and how to mitigate the performance impact of slower NVM accesses (compared to DRAM), most NVM indexes also leverage DRAM to store the reconstructible part of the index structure (such as inner nodes) in DRAM. Some even (e.g., DPTree) store entire trees (as part of the index) in DRAM.

Design Principle 1: Store reconstructible part of the index in DRAM.

The tradeoff is instant recovery as the DRAM-resident part needs to be rebuilt upon recovery. For node layout, using unsorted leaf nodes, fingerprinting and indirection are the most common design choices, regardless of whether the index is B+-tree or trie based. Using unsorted leaf nodes avoids extra write operations upon inserts (since keys are not always kept sorted). Fingerprinting further skips unnecessary reads by ending the probing operation early for keys that do not exist during negative search or existence check operations.

Table 6.2: Concurrency control and NVM management approaches in range NVM indexes. Optimistic approaches are commonly used and PMDK is arguably the standard in practice. Taken from [3], published under CC BY-NC-ND 4.0, reprinted with permission.

	Concurrency Control	NVM Management
wB+-Tree	N/A: single-threaded	Emulation first, then PMDK
BzTree	Lock-free (PMwCAS [7])	Emulation first, then PMDK
FPTree	HTM (inner) + locking (leaf)	PMDK with customization
NV-Tree	Locking	Emulation first, then PMDK
LB+-Tree	HTM (inner) + locking (leaf)	PMDK with customization
DPTree	Optimistic locking + asynchronous updates	PMDK
ROART	Optimistic locking (ROWEX)	PMDK with customization
PACTree	Optimistic locking + asynchronous updates	PMDK with customization
APEX	Optimistic locking	PMDK

Design Principle 2: Add additional metadata (e.g., fingerprints) and loosen node/bucket sortedness to skip unnecessary NVM reads and writes.

The tradeoff for using unsorted nodes is the performance of operations that need sorted key order (e.g., range scans). Indirection is an effective approach to maintaining sorted order of keys without having to shift actual key-value data.

All of the Optane-era indexes are also designed to use index nodes/buckets that are of multiples of physical NVM access granularity, i.e., 256-byte for Optane PMem. Such optimizations are often necessary to exploit the full potential of the hardware (similar to making B+ trees cache-conscious by aligning node sizes to multiples of cacheline sizes). However, we do not categorize this as a new principle because it is already commonplace in memory-centric index design and specific to one product.

6.3 Concurrency

In terms of concurrency control, as we summarize in Table 6.2, none of the NVM indexes use traditional pessimistic locking or traditional lock coupling. Rather, they all use some flavour of optimistic locking based on version verification, or lock-free approaches that provide strong progress guarantees. For example, BzTree uses a persistent multi-word compare-and-swap (PMwCAS) [7] primitive to achieve both lock-free behaviour and easy implementation. The main benefit of using optimistic/lock-free approaches is that reads (e.g., index probing which is fundamental for any index) do not usually incur shared memory (NVM) writes, leading to high performance and good scalability for read-mostly workloads which are very common in practice.

> *Design Principle 3:* Avoid pessimistic concurrency control (e.g., traditional lock coupling).

Hardware transactional memory (HTM) is also used by certain indexes. However, as related work has noted [3], HTM presents several drawbacks and challenges. (1) It requires special hardware support, yet most modern processors (especially Intel ones) and OS (including Linux kernel) disable HTM by default for security concerns. (2) As a result, using HTM will add more development cost in software as developers have to explicitly change system-wide settings to enable it (e.g., by modifying Linux bootup parameters), and may open up security risks. (3) In its current form, HTM presents many limitations, such as limited footprint size and poor performance under contention; both require careful considerations at design time. These all make it hard for HTM-based approaches to be adopted in practice. In comparison, optimistic locking approaches are pure software and easy to implement. Solutions now also already exist for handle high-contention workloads and mitigate the unfairness between reads and writes [1, 6], which are drawbacks of traditional optimistic locks. It is therefore expected that future indexes to continue to use optimistic concurrency.

6.4 NVM Management

Managing NVM is a non-trivial task for NVM indexes. With much research (e.g., those mentioned in Chapter 2) and industry effort, various NVM programming libraries provide a comprehensive set of tools for developers to use. In particular, at least for the surveyed indexes, the Persistent Memory Development Kit (PMDK) [4] has become the de-facto standard for handling NVM management issues, such as allocation/deallocation and avoiding permanent memory leaks. However, many proposals also devised further optimizations on top of vanilla PMDK which often does not provide the best performance. For example, PACTree devises a NUMA-aware design as PMDK itself does not provide such functionality. FPTree used more coarse-grained allocations from PMDK allocator to reduce allocation costs.

> *Design Principle 4:* Enhance NVM management on top of existing allocators to ease bottlenecks while avoiding persistent memory leaks.

A similar parallel is the current state of standard `malloc` implementations in the standard C library: Although a standard library exists, high-performance systems still usually require better allocators (such as `jemalloc` [2]) to fit their needs.

References

[1] Böttcher, J., Leis, V., Giceva, J., Neumann, T., Kemper, A.: Scalable and Robust Latches for Database Systems. In: Proceedings of the 16th International Workshop on Data Management on New Hardware, DaMoN '20. Association for Computing Machinery, New York, NY, USA (2020)

[2] Evans, J.: A Scalable Concurrent malloc (3) Implementation for FreeBSD. In: Proceedings of the BSDCan Conference (2006)

[3] He, Y., Lu, D., Huang, K., Wang, T.: Evaluating Persistent Memory Range Indexes: Part Two. Proc. VLDB Endow. **15**(11), 2477–2490 (2022)

[4] Intel: Persistent Memory Development Kit (2021). URL `http://pmem.io/pmdk`. Last accessed: June 7, 2022

[5] Lersch, L., Hao, X., Oukid, I., Wang, T., Willhalm, T.: Evaluating Persistent Memory Range Indexes. PVLDB **13**(4), 574–587 (2019)

[6] Shi, G., Yan, Z., Wang, T.: OptiQL: Robust Optimistic Locking for Memory-Optimized Indexes. In: Proceedings of the 2024 ACM SIGMOD International Conference on Management of Data, SIGMOD '24 (2024)

[7] Wang, T., Levandoski, J., Larson, P.A.: Easy lock-free indexing in non-volatile memory. In: 2018 IEEE 34th International Conference on Data Engineering (ICDE), pp. 461–472 (2018)

Chapter 7
Lessons Learned and Outlook

Abstract This final chapter discusses the "lessons learned" from previous research on NVM indexing and gives an outlook to future NVM indexing and indexing techniques in general. We analyze the potential reasons for the demise of Optane PMem, followed by the "legacy" left by NVM-based indexes discussed in previous chapters, and potential future work.

7.1 A Cautionary Tale of Optane PMem

The commercialization of Optane PMem enabled perhaps at least two thirds of our discussions thus far. It has set the de-facto standards for almost every aspect of NVM:

- **Hardware Requirements:** The memory controller in the CPU needs to support both types of memory (DRAM and PMem), and present to software address ranges of NVM and ordinary volatile DRAM. Additional CPU instructions such as CLWB and CLFLUSHOPT are added for software to ensure data persistence in PMem. Also, the support of ADR and eADR paved ways for designing future NVM architectures.
- **Programming Models:** The programming model specifies how NVM applications such as indexes should be built. With the given hardware support, Intel developed a series of software tools and libraries such as ndctl and PMDK to manage and develop software for Optane PMem. While other approaches exist, practically all research and industry projects are using these tools or some variants of them.

In terms of delivering the NVM vision illustrated in the beginning of this book, Optane was the first successful product (at least to some degree) that delivered all the three desirable properties of high capacity (e.g., up to 12TB per machine which rivals flash SSDs), sub-microsecond level latency (~300ns which is not too far away from DRAM compared to flash memory) and persistence in the DDR form factor.

K. Huang, T. Wang, *Indexing on Non-Volatile Memory*, SpringerBriefs in Computer Science, https://doi.org/10.1007/978-3-031-47627-3_7

All of these were extremely exciting when Optane PMem was first announced in 2015 and finally released in 2019 because the research community and industry had been using DRAM-based emulation for over a decade. As more efforts were put into developing software for the Optane PMem eco-system, however, it became clear to researchers and practitioners that two inter-related major hurdles are blocking the wide adoption of Optane PMem: high cost compared to flash memory and low performance relative to DRAM. There are also non-technical reasons which we will discuss in the following analysis.

7.1.1 Total Cost of Acquisition

Cost plays an important role in determining whether a breakthrough technology such as Optane can gain wide adoption. Here we focus on the total cost of acquisition (TCA)[1] of Optane PMem-based systems and present a representative comparison with traditional SSD-based servers.[2] For fair comparison, our analysis takes a baseline server with the same components except the "storage" media. The PMem-based configuration uses Optane PMem to realize the "NVM vision" where PMem is both the working memory and storage for persistent data structures (such as indexes). It does not have to be equipped with other secondary storage devices, such as SSDs. Although in practice this is often the case, to ease comparison we do not consider them here. The SSD-based configuration is the familiar "DRAM-SSD" architecture where persistent data structures are durably stored in SSD and cached by DRAM; no PMem is present in the system.

Considered Components and Metrics. Let us first consider what needs to be included in the TCA of a server, in addition to PMem DIMMs and SSDs. First, CPU is necessary as it dictates data movement logic. More importantly, for PMem-based systems the CPU is also the major unit that accomplishes data movement using synchronous `load` and `store` instructions.[3] In contrast, a DRAM-SSD system uses asynchronous DMA for actual data movement and the CPU only needs to manage control flow. As we shall see soon, this difference has profound impact on cost. Second, it is clear that for a traditional SSD-based system DRAM cost must be considered. Even in PMem-based systems, however, DRAM is necessary due to limitations on how Optane PMem must be deployed. We therefore consider CPU, DRAM and the storage media (PMem or SSD) in our analysis.

Deployment Restrictions. Both PMem and SSD servers require some population rules for CPU, DRAM and the storage device itself. That is, in order to put up a working server, the server configuration must be equipped with a certain number of CPU and DRAM DIMMs. Otherwise the machine may not even boot up. The requirements for putting up a traditional SSD storage server is pretty straightforward.

---

[1] As opposed to TCO (total cost of ownership) which may include factors such as operational costs.

[2] Based on prior work by Huang et al. [6] where interested readers may find more details.

[3] Later generations of hardware are adding asynchronous semantics for memory [4], but they are not widely used yet as of this writing.

The machine can be configured with almost an arbitrary non-zero amount of CPU, DRAM and SSDs. There is no specific requirements for pairing the number of SSDs and DRAM DIMMs. The cost of CPU (number of CPU cores dedicated to handling I/O) is also low, because as mentioned earlier it is mainly for control flow.

However, for PMem the rules are more restrictive, with specific requirements on the number of DRAM DIMMs vs. the number of PMem DIMMs. For example, it is required that each controller must be equipped at least one DRAM DIMM for the PMem on the same controller to work. In other words, a PMem-based system still has to be equipped with DRAM. Further, PMem DIMMs in fact run at a lower frequency (e.g., 2999MT/s) than DDR DRAM. When they are present in the same system, this means the entire memory subsystem frequency needs to be clocked down, affecting overall memory performance. Finally, PMem relies on the CPU's load and store instructions for data movement (whereas SSDs can use asynchronous DMA), driving up the number of needed CPU cores. Especially, PMem requires higher-end (hence more expensive) Intel CPU models, further driving up the overall cost. In contrast, none of these were required by SSD servers: they can use almost any CPU or DRAM configurations as the application workloads see fit. The result is then PMem-based servers often overprovision precious CPU and DRAM resources.

TCA Comparison. With the qualitative analysis above, now we take a closer look at the cost per GB for PMem and SSD based systems using concrete examples. For fair comparison, we take a dual-socket server with two 20-core Intel Xeon Gold 6242R CPUs. The CPU cost is then prorated based on the needed number of cores to saturate PMem/SSD or reach desirable throughput/IOPS. We then vary its DRAM and storage media (either Optane PMem 100 series or Optane P4800X SSD). Note that we use the Optane P4800X SSD which is also based on the same (generation of) Optane media, but is in the PCIe form factor.[4] That is, it presents the same block interface as flash SSDs and hard disks. The use of an Optane-based SSD makes the comparison particularly interesting as it allows us to see how cost/performance metrics can change drastically due to differences in form factors for the same physical storage material.

Table 7.1 shows five configurations considered in our analysis using prices from public sources [6]. In the table, PMn represents a configuration with n PMem DIMMs, and P4800Xm represents a configuration with m P4800X SSDs. Per GB (without CPU) highlights the additional cost of DRAM, compared to Per GB (storage only) which only considers the storage media (PMem or P4800X). The other per GB numbers take into consideration the amount of CPU cycles that may be required to saturate the storage component. P4800X1 and P4800X2 require only a single thread to saturate the drive(s) and exhibit the lowest costs (Per GB with 1 thread). PMem configurations usually require more threads which drive up the per GB cost (Per GB with 1/5/10 threads) by up to over 4× (PM1 with ten threads vs. P4800X2 with one thread).

Based on the table, we highlight several findings. First, being in DDR memory form factor alone drives the cost of PMem up as the "storage only" numbers have

---

[4] Recall from Chapter 2 that NVM can be used to build both memory and block storage devices.

Table 7.1: Cost (USD) of five server configurations (as of September 2021) with different numbers of PMem DIMMs and SSDs. Taken from [6], published under CC-BY 4.0.

Component	PM1	PM4	PM6	P4800X1	P4800X2
CPU (1×Intel Xeon Gold 6242R)	$2,517	$2,517	$2,517	$2,517	$2,517
DDR4 DRAM (6×32GB)	$1,157.94	$1,157.94	$1,157.94	$1,157.94	$1,157.94
Optane PMem (n×128GB)	$546.75	$2,187.00	$3,280.50	N/A	N/A
Optane SSD P4800X (m×375GB)	N/A	N/A	N/A	$999	$1,998
Total	$4,221.69	$5,861.94	$6,955.44	$4,673.94	$5,672.94
Per GB (storage-only)	$4.27	$4.27	$4.27	$2.66	$2.66
Per GB without CPU	$13.32	$6.53	$5.78	$5.75	$4.21
Per GB with full CPU	$32.98	$11.45	$9.06	$12.46	$7.56
Per GB with 1 thread	$13.81	$6.66	$5.86	$5.92	$4.29
Per GB with 5 threads	$15.78	$7.15	$6.19	N/A	N/A
Per GB with 10 threads	$18.23	$7.76	$6.60	N/A	N/A

shown. Second, although the cost per GB of Optane PMem is lower than that of DRAM, when we add the necessary CPU and DRAM costs, the overall cost for PMem servers becomes much higher than SSD servers. In other words, the CPU and DRAM costs can subvert the cost-effectiveness of PMem, which was part of the reason why many applications wanted to adopt NVM in the first place. The only way to amortize this cost is to add more PMem DIMMs to the system, however, this may again risk overprovisioning and would only pay off if the application indeed needs more PMem capacity. Finally, since PMem is in DDR memory form factor, it naturally needs to occupy (precious) memory slots and channels, which are very limited resources on the motherboard. The system designer then needs to very carefully decide on the amount of DRAM and PMem to have on a server. Yet SSD servers are usually much more expandable. It is not uncommon to see high-end systems feature tens of storage ports with the number of supported SSDs decoupled with the memory subsystem.

7.1.2 Performance Per Dollar

Given the relative high cost and deployment complexity, it then becomes paramount for PMem to deliver high performance or low cost per performance. Based on the TCA costs above, we now look at how cost per performance of PMem- and SSD-based servers would compare. There could be many different ways in choosing the workloads and applications. Because of the focus of this book is NVM indexing, we describe the approach and results of our prior work [6] that compares two classic NVM indexes (FPTree [10] and BzTree [3]) and a textbook implementation of SSD-based B+-tree that uses a simple buffer pool in DRAM. As we have already introduced in Chapter 4, FPTree and BzTree are tailored for NVM with many optimizations.

The SSD-based B+-tree, on the contrary, was not optimized as much as FPTree and BzTree, without even using any asynchronous I/O primitives; instead, it uses the synchronous `pread` and `pwrite` interfaces. To test the performance of these two indexes, we pick several representative workloads that involve point queries and inserts of 8-byte keys and 8-byte values. The index is initialized with 100 million key-value pairs. With this setup, we measure the performance of FPTree, BzTree and the on-SSD B+-tree using the aforementioned configurations such as PM1, PM4, etc. For SSD configurations, we vary the percentage of buffered data compared to total data size, represented by N%M which means the buffer pool size is set to N% of the data. After getting the raw performance numbers, we calculate the performance per dollar metric as follows [6]:

$$R = \frac{P}{\$S + \$D + \$E} = \frac{P}{\$S + \$D + (W * U) * (\$C * \frac{1}{T})} \tag{7.1}$$

In the equation, performance per dollar (R) is measured by throughput (P) divided by the cost (in USD) of the required hardware resources, including the storage device cost (S), DRAM cost (D) and CPU cost (E). It is relatively straightforward to derive S and D but trickier to determine $\$E$. We deduced it from several factors:

- W: the number of worker threads used to run the experiment;
- U: average CPU utilization during the experiment which represents the CPU cycles used for data movement;
- C: price to purchase the entire CPU;
- T: number of total hardware threads provided by the CPU.

Among these parameters, it is necessary to include U because SSD-based systems (P4800X1 here) often do not use all the CPU cores for I/O. Rather, CPU is mainly for computation after data is loaded into memory (DRAM). In particular, for P4800X1 it ranges from ~10 to 100% (when all the data is buffered) as SSD I/O is blocking in nature and can use asynchronous DMA for data transfer. For NVM indexes (FPTree and BzTree) it is 100% for FPTree and BzTree because NVM uses synchronous memory instructions to move data. As a result, $U \times W$ will give the "effective" number of threads needed by a workload. With the CPU price C, C/T will give the per-thread cost.

Figure 7.1 shows the raw performance and performance per dollar results. Note that here the SSD server has only one P4800X SSD. So a fair comparison would be with PM1, although we also show the results for PM4 and PM6. Compared to FPTree, the SSD B+-tree exhibits very high raw performance and performance/cost ratio for read-only workloads under both skewed and uniform key access patterns when all the data is cached (B+Tree-100%). This means if the workload in fact fits in DRAM (i.e., DRAM capacity is not a concern) but still requires persistence, the SSD system will provide both high performance and low cost per performance. When the workload does not fit in memory anymore, we see that SSD B+-tree performs similarly to PM1 under 90% buffer pool hit ratio and can even outperform PM1 when the hit ratio is 80%. NVM's advantage is mainly shown for the insert workloads in Figures 7.1(c) and (f) when there is enough bandwidth under PM4 and

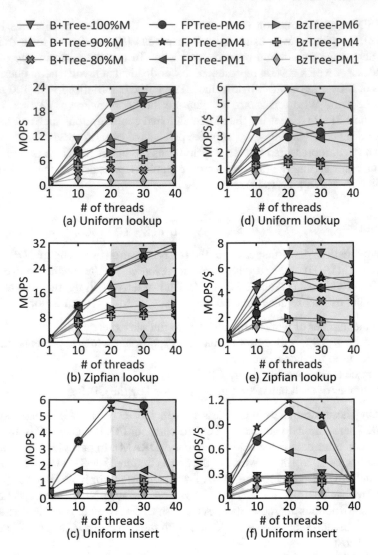

Fig. 7.1: Throughput (million operations per second) (a–c) and performance/cost ratios (d–f) of range indexes. Taken from [6], published under CC-BY 4.0.

PM6. Under PM1, BzTree still gives lower performance and cost per performance than SSD-based B+-tree. Overall, the observation is that PMem's performance is better demonstrated when there is enough PMem DIMMs, which in turn will require more CPU cores dedicated to moving data and potentially more DRAM to accommodate for the configuration requirements. This unfortunately can drive up TCA and trade off performance per dollar. For an SSD based system, however, there is much less (if any) coupling between the SSD, CPU and DRAM, allowing it to provide overall very good performance per dollar metrics. We have only shown the cases for tree-based indexes here. For more details with NVM hash table vs. SSD hash tables, interested readers may refer to the work by Huang et al. [6].

7.1.3 Non-Technical Factors

In addition to the technical factors mentioned above, we observe several non-technical factors that we suspect have also contributed to the demise of Optane PMem. We hope these factors can be considered seriously for future NVM ecosystems.

Single-Vendor. One of the major pain points for adopting Optane PMem is that there is only a single manufacturer, Intel. Although the technology was initially co-developed by Micron and Intel, the only commercially available product was from Intel. This can lead to much uncertainty and higher risk for software vendors: hardware pricing will largely be dictated by a single company, and developers will in essence develop products based on a single device. The latter can eventually make building NVM-based software a niche area, driving up developer costs for software vendors, eventually leading to lower competitiveness of PMem-based products compared to for example SSD-based systems. Further, it can make software vendors become more reluctant to build PMem-based systems and end up in a vicious cycle.

Closed Ecosystem. Related to the previous issue, although the Optane PMem devices are built in DDR form factor, it requires changes in the memory controller which is usually part of the CPU itself in modern systems. Again, the only platforms that support Optane PMem were from Intel. Other CPU vendors (e.g., AMD and ARM) did not support Optane PMem. This leads to the same vicious cycles mentioned above. Although as a third-party we do not have clear details on why the ecosystem is closed, it is reasonable to suspect that had the Optane PMem DIMMs can be used on other platforms, such as AMD or ARM, there may have been more widespread adoption.

7.2 Lessons Learned

Based on the above analysis, we summarize several lessons learned that we hope can be useful for future work.

Open Ecosystem. An open ecosystem would allow more vendors to get into the market and innovate at a faster speed. Unlike having a single vendor, this would allow more competition and benefit customers with richer feature sets and lower price, eventually leading to more adoption of future potential NVM technologies.

Fewer Deployment Restrictions. As we can see from the TCA and performance/-cost ratio analysis, a major reason that drives down the performance/cost ratio is that for an Optane PMem server to work, a considerable amount of CPU cycles and

DRAM need to be (over)provisioned. Future NVM products should reduce such restrictions. After all, the original NVM vision even allows no DRAM at all.

Software Design Should be General. Perhaps over half of the techniques covered in this book were tailored for Optane PMem. While it is necessary to be hardware-conscious for performance reasons, it is important to also consider forward compatibility when designing future NVM indexes, given that the exact performance characteristics of future NVM is unclear at the moment.

Pay More Attention to Functionality. One of the major common issues in many NVM indexing proposals we have discussed so far is that they try to optimize for the "low hanging fruit" workloads while ignoring other critical features. For example, all the mentioned indexes would test using 8-byte keys and 8-byte values, yet very few of them ever considered longer or variable-length keys which are more common in practice. Another example is NUMA awareness which again only very few indexes considered. Future NVM indexes (and indexes in general) should (re)focus their attention to these issues.

7.3 Outlook

So far, it seems that our analysis in this chapter has painted a very bleak picture about NVM indexing: NVM performance is still much slower than that of DRAM, the only commercial device is cancelled after many years of expectation, the performance/cost ratio does not always look favourable, and other NVM device candidates are still in the works without a clear path to commercialization or mass production. While all of these are true, we make three important observations which are leading to promising further development of the area.

7.3.1 NVM Indexing Techniques for DRAM Indexing

As discussed previously, a fundamentally design principle of current NVM indexes is to reduce the amount unnecessary NVM accesses (reads and writes). Similarly, when the indexing structure is DRAM or SSD resident, these techniques could also apply to reduce DRAM/SSD accesses. For example, fingerprinting in FPTree and LB$^+$-Tree allows negative search operations to end early. The same technique can also be applied in DRAM-based indexes, such as ART [7] and Masstree [8]. Another example is the use of unsorted nodes and subsequently linear searching during node traversal. This was originally a tradeoff for NVM indexes: since keeping records in index nodes sorted will usually involve shifting key-value positions, one may simply not keep the keys in a node sorted, but only append keys/values. The tradeoff is then searching within a node becomes linear and so the node should not be too big, to maintain reasonable performance. This is a very popular design in NVM indexes, yet coincidentally, it is desirable for DRAM-based to also not use very large nodes for better CPU cache locality. Linear search is often even faster anyway than binary search because the latter may incur more cache misses. In this context, using unsorted nodes becomes an obvious optimization that could further improve performance by removing key shifting overheads in DRAM.

Recent work [5] has taken the first step to evaluate the potential of these NVM techniques on DRAM, by running representative NVM indexes (e.g., FPTree) on DRAM with the cacheline flush and extra memory fence instructions removed. The results showed very competitive and sometimes even better performance than indexes that are heavily optimized for DRAM. Therefore, adapting and exploring NVM indexing techniques for DRAM is a promising future direction.

7.3.2 Leveraging NVDIMMs

NVDIMMs built with traditional materials (DRAM and flash memory) have been standardized and commercially available (from multiple vendors) for many years. Especially, several research projects have assumed NVDIMM-N (e.g., BzTree [3]) before Optane PMem became available. Some real products also already use them. For example, SQL Server uses NVDIMMs to store the log buffer for fast transaction commit [9]. Just like "true" NVM built with new materials, NVDIMMs also exhibit a wide range of performance characteristics: NVDIMM-N promises the same runtime performance as DRAM, whereas others such as NVDIMM-F is slower because it only uses DRAM as a transparent cache in front of flash memory, presenting the system a larger but slower main memory. It is still yet to be explored by the software research community on how exactly to leverage these properties. With Optane PMem winding down, it is plausible that NVDIMMs may (again) become the a hardware platform (other than retired Optane platforms) for NVM research, similar to what it was before Optane PMem was released. Recent work has already started to leverage some of the properties. For example, NV-SQL [2] shows how a small NVDIMM-N device can drastically improve OLTP performance in a traditional storage-centric DBMS assuming the DRAM-SSD architecture. We expect such devices to receive more attention, or at least as a stop-gap solution, before next-generation NVM and far-memory technologies become a reality.

7.3.3 Future NVM and Far Memory Technologies

There are already several promising future NVM candidates in the works. As we have covered in Chapter 2, they exhibit quite different performance characteristics, some of which may invalidate the central assumption made by the indexing techniques in the last three chapters. For example, STT-MRAM could offer lower latency than DRAM with persistence and replace SRAM and DRAM all the way down. This would mean the storage hierarchy could become more homogeneous. Existing indexes that try to save NVM accesses by adding more complex logic then may or may not still be profitable as the extra compute itself could become expensive. Again, since these new technologies are still in early stages, it remains to be seen how exactly they will develop in the coming years, and whether they will be able to deliver the "NVM vision" without falling into such traps as a closed ecosystem and high TCA.

Complementary to the NVM vision is the direction of resource disaggregation where storage and memory are both disaggregated from compute (CPU). In such architectures, memory, storage, and compute elements all form their own clusters (pools) that are interconnected via high-speed, cache-coherent (where applicable) interconnects such as the Compute Express Link (CXL) [1]. One of the major benefits of disaggregation is to allow elasticity and independent scalability of each type of resource. In contrast, in a traditional server the amount of CPU cores, DRAM and storage is fixed once the server is configured: Overprovisioning would drive up the cost, while under-provisioning would not satisfy application needs. In a disaggregated environment, application logic is deployed in the compute cluster to leverage elastic compute resources and memory/storage can expand or shrink as needed. The ability to disaggregated CPU and memory mitigates one of the aforementioned drawbacks of PMem where NVM DIMMs and DRAM DIMMs compete for the limited memory controller bandwidth and DDR slots. However, the storage hierarchy also become more diverse, with local memory, remote memory, local storage (e.g., SSD) and remote storage. Since remote memory access latency is still much longer than local DRAM latency, reducing unnecessary accesses to remote memory again becomes important. This means the same idea of retrofitting NVM indexing techniques to a similar environment (this time remote memory) will apply again.

References

[1] Compute Express Link™: The breakthrough cpu-to-device interconnect (2023). URL https://www.computeexpresslink.org/
[2] An, M., Park, J., Wang, T., Nam, B., Lee, S.W.: NV-SQL: Boosting OLTP Performance with Non-Volatile DIMMs. Proc. VLDB Endow. **16**(6), 1453–1465 (2023)
[3] Arulraj, J., Levandoski, J.J., Minhas, U.F., Larson, P.: BzTree: A High-Performance Latch-free Range Index for Non-Volatile Memory. PVLDB **11**(5), 553–565 (2018)
[4] Balcer, P.: Leveraging asynchronous hardware accelerators for fun and profit (2022). URL https://pmem.io/blog/2022/02/leveraging-asynchronous-hardware-accelerators-for-fun-and-profit
[5] He, Y., Lu, D., Huang, K., Wang, T.: Evaluating Persistent Memory Range Indexes: Part Two. Proc. VLDB Endow. **15**(11), 2477–2490 (2022)
[6] Huang, K., Imai, D., Wang, T., Xie, D.: SSDs Striking Back: The Storage Jungle and Its Implications on Persistent Indexes. In: 12th Annual Conference

on Innovative Data Systems Research, CIDR 2022, Chaminade, CA, USA, January 9-12, 2022, Online Proceedings (2022)

[7] Leis, V., Kemper, A., Neumann, T.: The Adaptive Radix Tree: ARTful Indexing for Main-Memory Databases. In: Proceedings of the 2013 IEEE International Conference on Data Engineering, ICDE '13, p. 38–49 (2013)

[8] Mao, Y., Kohler, E., Morris, R.T.: Cache Craftiness for Fast Multicore Key-Value Storage. In: Proceedings of the 7th ACM european conference on Computer Systems, pp. 183–196 (2012)

[9] Microsoft: Transaction Commit latency acceleration using Storage Class Memory in Windows Server 2016/SQL Server 2016 SP1 (2016). URL https://learn.microsoft.com/en-ca/archive/blogs/sqlserverstorageengine/transaction-commit-latency-acceleration-using-storage-class-memory-in-windows-server-2016sql-server-2016-sp1

[10] Oukid, I., Lasperas, J., Nica, A., Willhalm, T., Lehner, W.: FPTree: A Hybrid SCM-DRAM Persistent and Concurrent B-Tree for Storage Class Memory. In: Proceedings of the 2016 International Conference on Management of Data, SIGMOD '16, p. 371–386. Association for Computing Machinery, New York, NY, USA (2016)

Printed in the United States
by Baker & Taylor Publisher Services